"When I met Jess over a decade [ago, she was a] believer still carrying a lot of hurt [from her past. While] the pain is still part of her story, t[oday it no longer de]fines her present and secures her [future. Having expe]rienced indescribable emptiness from getting caught up in the false promises of the world, *Face Off with Your Feelings* is a powerful testimony of how Jesus radically transformed Jess's life—and how He offers you the same hope."

    Michelle Myers, cofounder of *She Works His Way*

"With a mix of science, psychology, theology, and good old life experience, Jessica has taken a complex subject and brought integration and clarity to it! The tie between our healing and the spirit, soul, body, and emotions is so real and there haven't been many brave enough to take it on with the care that she has. I appreciate the clear way that she explains what is going on and then practical ways to implement and make some headway in our lives! This book will be not just a help for you personally but a resource that you pass on to many!"

    Clare Smith, writer/speaker/blogger at *claresmith.me*

"In *Face Off with Your Feelings*, Jessica Hottle is a gentle mentor and friend who will walk alongside you in this stressed-out, pain-filled world that we live in. If emotional healing feels impossible for you, and past pain keeps resurfacing, you'll find empowering, helpful, and biblical guidance here. This kind, thoughtful book will help you find your way, ultimately leading you toward a safe place with God."

    Jennifer Dukes Lee, author of *Growing Slow* and *It's All Under Control*

"Jessica invites you in to have the messy but needed conversation around healing that is required to grow past the hurt and live free. By the end you will feel seen, understood, comforted, and equipped with tangible tools to help you create space for healing, grow closer to the Lord, understand your feelings and emotions without condemnation, and move toward intentional healing. Jessica breaks down complex neuroscience topics in a way that the everyday woman can grasp, and intertwines it with Scripture truths to point us back to Christ—our Creator, Comforter, and Hope. If you want to live a transformed life mentally, physically, and spiritually, this is a must read. I will be recommending this book to everyone I come across."

  Clara Norfleet, registered dietitian nutritionist and author of *Simple Staples*

"Jessica Hottle's latest book, *Face Off with Your Feelings*, is a must-read! I was captured from the opening sentence. I've learned a new way to heal on my spiritual journey and find myself equipped to speak against the lies I've told myself for so long. If you're ready to do the emotional work but don't know how, this book is for you!"

  Erin Youngblood, founder of *The Clean Campaign, Inc.*

"*Face Off with Your Feelings* is a power-packed resource for those dreaming of true healing. Jess brings to life the truth that God says about Himself and what He says about His most prized possessions; messy, broken, us. Jess's life is a testimony of His grace and what His love can transform. There is hope for today! There is hope in God's gracious healing. You will, undoubtedly, be blessed by Jess's words in this book!"

  Emily Copeland, pastor's wife and author

"'No one is here to hurt you. God is taking care of you.' This line stuck with me as I read every word of *Face Off with Your Feelings*. God's words through Jess are powerful and the way she connects your spirit, soul, and body while intentionally pointing you to the Word of God is necessary. You may think you don't 'need this book,' but I promise you—you *need* this book. We all have parts of our lives that need continued healing, and I love how Jess not only helps you recognize those areas but walks with you through understanding the hurt and intentionally healing. Not just pushing it to the side but truly diving in and walking away *transformed.*"

Caroline Foster, founder of *Fit for His Glory*

"This isn't a book written by someone or for someone who's looking for a quick fix. This book is gentle and kind as it also allows for the raw and real. You can always count on Jess to give whole truths because she's a woman who spends time with God. In *Face Off with Your Feelings*, you will learn how to battle your feelings well, without the sting of fear or shame. If you're a child of God or even willing to consider what that means, an excellent resource for living a healthy and whole life now lies in your hands."

Alisa Keeton, founder, *Revelation Wellness*; author, *The Wellness Revelation* and *Heir to the Crown*

Face Off
with your
Feelings

Break Up with the Lies of Your Past and
Embrace the Truth for Your Future

JESSICA HOTTLE

Copyright © 2021 Jessica Hottle

All rights reserved, including the right to reproduce this book or portions of this book in any form whatsoever without the prior written permission of the copyright holder.

Scripture quotations, unless otherwise indicated, are from the New King James Version®. Copyright © 1982 by Thomas Nelson. Used by permission. All rights reserved.

Scripture quotations marked AMP are taken from the Amplified® Bible, Copyright © 2015 by The Lockman Foundation. Used by permission. www.Lockman.org.

Scripture quotations marked ESV are taken from the ESV® Bible (The Holy Bible, English Standard Version®), copyright © 2001 by Crossway, a publishing ministry of Good News Publishers. Used by permission. All rights reserved.

Scripture quotations marked KJV are taken from the Authorized Version, or King James Version, of the Bible.

Scripture quotations marked TLB are taken from *The Living Bible* copyright© 1971. Used by permission of Tyndale House Publishers, Inc., Carol Stream, Illinois 60188. All rights reserved.

Scripture quotations marked MSG are taken from *The Message*. Copyright©1993, 2002, 2018 by Eugene H. Peterson. Used by permission of NavPress. All rights reserved. Represented by Tyndale House Publishers, a Division of Tyndale House Ministries.

This book depicts actual events in the life of the author as truthfully as recollection permits and/or can be verified by research. Occasionally, dialogue consistent with the character or nature of the person speaking has been supplemented. All persons within are actual individuals; there are no composite characters. The names of some individuals have been changed to respect their privacy.

Limits of Liability and Disclaimer of Warranty
The author and publisher shall not be liable for your misuse of this material. This book is strictly for informational and educational purposes.

The purpose of this book is to educate and entertain. The author and/or publisher does not guarantee that anyone following these techniques, suggestions, tips, ideas, or strategies will become successful. The author and/or publisher shall have neither liability nor responsibility to anyone with respect to any loss or damage caused, or alleged to be caused, directly or indirectly by the information contained in this book

Cover by Chloe Creative Studio
Art by Jacob Hottle

To the ones who feel like they are on a constant emotional roller coaster and don't know how to get off, allow your theme song to be of faith, patience, and time. Healing requires faith in Jesus, patience in the process, and time to renew your mind as you rebuild the narratives you have believed for too long.

Jon, thank you for loving me the way you do. You handle my feelings with care and always challenge me in them. I am so grateful for you. I love you.

Contents

Introduction *1*

1. Creating Space for Healing 11
2. The Identity Effect 23
3. Discerning the Truth 39
4. The Healing Connection 55
5. Addressing Your Whole Self 67
6. Understanding Feelings and Emotions 83
7. Changing Your Mind 97
8. The Rework 115
9. Emotional Safety 127
10. Intentional Healing 143

Acknowledgments *157*
About the Author *159*

Introduction

I saw her name pop up on my phone while I was walking on the treadmill: Rachel. Fear slammed into me as if I hit a brick wall going a hundred miles an hour. Then uneasiness settled deep in my bones as my stomach twisted into knots. My heart was beating hard and fast. I could hear my heartbeat in my ears like drums beating at a steady tempo. In a matter of moments, the wind was knocked out of me as I grabbed the side handrails and put my feet on each side of the treadmill belt. "Jess, breathe," I told myself. Why was I getting so worked up? Nothing was wrong. I was entirely safe. I began to regain my composure and collapsed on the couch. What had just happened?

After my body had time to relax, I wondered why Rachel's name had triggered this response in me. My reaction showed me trauma I did not know existed was still held within my body. Rachel was a close relative, and her actions and words led me to believe I would never amount to anything. Even though it was long in the past, seeing the name made everything I had experienced with her—the pain I had felt—buckle me at my knees. Worse, seeing her name made me wonder if I would have to be on guard and ready to protect myself at all costs for the rest of my life. Even though ten years have passed since I have seen Rachel, I can remember all the days spent with her as though they happened a few months ago.

That day on the treadmill, I learned my body is a great storyteller. Knowing this sent me on a quest to uncover and unpack the moments of my life that built layers of concrete walls around my heart. Whether we are consciously thinking of our hard stories or those days spent with the person or not, our bodies don't forget. Our bodies become our protectors. The body we carry throughout our day knows the pain and history and will try to protect us from repeating the cycle. Our bodies will put up defenses to prepare us for when/if that type of pain or situation happens again.

As time went on, I learned that I formed a belief about Rachel, me, and the unhealthy situation we were in together every time I was with her. This pain, anger, and resentment chipped away at my foundation until it was crumbling, and I believed I was a failure—a failure to myself and my body.

I wrestled my feelings of inadequacy and felt as though I would never live up to what people wanted or expected of me. For example, the people in my life and around me wanted me to be at their beck and call.

When they needed something from me, I was supposed to be there, no matter what it cost me. The men I dated wanted my body to look different, or for me to act or dress a certain way. If I questioned them, I was the one in the wrong. Most days became a fight to be heard and seen for who I was and not what people expected of me. The battle I fought was within myself and separate from my heavenly Father. He was the one who could release me from my confinement and condemnation that were the foundation of my identity. He could give me the pieces to rebuild the foundation. I wanted to be a woman of her word and a woman of integrity, and the journey with healing emotional scars became like digging up a treasure chest under three feet of concrete. Freedom in Christ was the treasure chest. The concrete became the years of pain that built up the wall I had around my heart, which felt impenetrable.

Why am I sharing all this with you?

To give you hope.

To tell you to keep fighting for your health.

To remind you not to settle for one doctor's opinion or diagnosis.

To remind you to stay persistent to see the fruit of healing in your life.

To remind you God gets the final say over your life, not anyone else (and He calls you His beloved child).

To encourage your heart that how you feel today does not have to be how you feel tomorrow or forever.

To let you know that your heart matters, and your body is a great storyteller of what's going on in your heart.

To remind you not to become influenced by the world.

To remind you God wants to see you well.

He created every piece of your body to work together, like a choreographed dance filled with delicate details and graceful precision. Your body knows what it needs to repair and take care of itself. Will you listen as the Holy Spirit guides you through the story your body believes?

The work you do with the Father as you tend to your soul with Him will become a part of your testimony. He wants to be a part of this healing journey. Every feeling or moment of pain should always lead you to Christ.

You are being invited to partner with Him, step into faith (not works), be brave enough to believe His Word, and stay focused on His Word when the enemy tries to uproot it from your heart.

Be kind to yourself in this process of healing.

The day on the treadmill when I saw Rachel's name pop up on the phone, I had to sit down, take a few moments to breathe, and bring myself back to the truth. That meant being aware of what thoughts I was allowing to creep into my mind and speaking kind words over my body. "Jess, you are no longer that teenage girl," "You are loved and safe right now. No one is here to hurt you," and "God is taking care of you" are a few of the phrases I repeated to remind myself of the truth and bring me back to reality.

Rachel left marks on my soul. I haven't talked to her in years. The distance, boundaries, and healing through the lies helped me manage seeing her name pop up after years of not communicating.

What to Expect

Here is what you can expect from reading this book: You will feel challenged, have mixed emotions, and feel torn between what you may have believed for so long and new revelations the Lord may have for you. Feeling challenged is good news. The last thing any of us needs is a book telling us what we think we need to hear. I don't want my stories and journey to be the only things that encourage you. I want to provide new insight into the Word that maybe you didn't see before. Allow the Scriptures to create hope for you in your heart and a vision of His future for you. Faith needs hope; they work together. Hopelessness is no longer something you need to experience or carry.

When you begin to move in the direction of truth and healing, change will seem hard. Uprooting the lies that God is against you, doesn't want you well, or is waiting for you to mess up will feel hard as you allow Him to love those lies out of you, especially if His love is not something you have learned to receive. You'll find yourself fighting to believe a new way, think a new thought, or imagine yourself as a well person. If you have ever wondered why change seems hard sometimes, there is a reason. Standing on God's Word seems harder because you have moved in the direction of faith and awakened the enemy to the fact that you are not taking his side anymore. When you stand on the Word, the enemy starts to ramp up his work: deceit, lies, and manipulation of God's Word.

When you move in the direction of healing, tension is there because chains are breaking. Keep pulling yourself away from the lies and into truth. Embrace your tension. Beyond the tension is transformation.

This book is for you if you need and want to experience healing in your life and freedom in your heart—healing from words spoken over you, healing from things done to you, understanding the present, and understanding what it means to have freedom in your life as you move through pain. Maybe you have found yourself disconnected from His presence for too long and you are ready to reconnect with Him. This book is also for you if you want a deeper, more intimate relationship with the Father. When you pursue the Father, He puts your feelings, pain, and situations into submission, meaning they are no longer what controls you.

Here is what this book is not. This book is not about giving to God so He can give to you, or about your works and all the things you can do to get God to save you. This is not a book of transactions to get the desired result.

I don't have all the answers. I do have my story and the

words the Father has shared with me to share with you. I'm writing this book to share God's Word with you in hope that you can experience the same kind of freedom I have. I feel like the woman at the well whom Jesus encountered. This woman left her waterpot after Jesus told her who she was and who He was. She ran back into her city and told the people about Him. The important piece of this scripture is that many Samaritans of the city believed in Him because the woman shared her testimony. After they urged Jesus to stay with them, they said to the woman, "Now we believe, not because of what you said, for we ourselves have heard Him and we know that this is indeed the Christ, the Savior of the world" (John 4:42).

They believed for themselves not because of what she said to them but because of what He said to them individually. Here is my point: You can hear the Word of God, receive fresh revelation, or learn something new from the Bible from someone else, but you must take responsibility to build your relationship with Him.

Like the woman who left her waterpot, I'm here to share the good news with you. I'm here to remind you the tension is real. The tension is warfare. We must never stop fighting.

The Goal

In this book, my goal is to uncover what God's will is for you. Hint: His will is for you to live an abundant life with a whole, well body and mind. Together we'll uncover the lies you may believe (which I, too, once believed) about healing, self-care, and what taking care of your soul means. I believe Him when He said He came to set the captives free.

> The Spirit of the Lord GOD is upon me,
> Because the LORD has anointed and commissioned me

> To bring good news to the humble and afflicted;
> He has sent me to bind up [the wounds of] the brokenhearted,
> To proclaim release [from confinement and condemnation] to the [physical and spiritual] captives
> And freedom to prisoners. (Isaiah 61:1 AMP)

Whatever you are chained to (in a physical or spiritual sense), Christ has come to break the chains off you. When you break chains emotionally, you realize you have a choice about what you hold on to, accept, or don't want to be a part of anymore. When you break the chains physically, you realize you are no longer bound to the title of a specific disease in your body. The disease is not your identity. Breaking spiritual chains allows you to see God's true nature and character, independent of the world's view.

You cannot build a relationship with God through someone else in this world. He created a direct pathway of connection through the Holy Spirit to you. At times, the relationship will feel messy. That's okay. You'll never be perfect in this world. You don't have to settle into everything that comes your way. Learning to discern or recognize what is good in the words you hear and to process through your emotions will become an adventure with the Father.

When I began my new way of thinking, change was tough. Far too many times, I tried to make sense of things and couldn't. Your brain wants to reason every experience and encounter you have in this life. If you are not careful, your brain's attempts to reason will begin to shut down the power of God at work within you. Read in Isaiah how God uses His Word to remind you that His ways are higher:

> "For My thoughts are not your thoughts,
> Nor are your ways My ways," says the LORD.
> "For as the heavens are higher than the earth,

So are My ways higher than your ways,
And My thoughts than your thoughts." (Isaiah 55:8–9)

Rationalizing what you see to make God's Word fit into your reality is bringing God down to your level instead of being obedient to God at a level you may not be able to comprehend. Second Peter 1:3 says, "His divine power has given to us all things that pertain to life and godliness, through the knowledge of Him who called us by glory and virtue." You can read this scripture and try to rationalize what you see in the moment. You may not feel like you have anything pertaining to life and godliness. You want answers, and you feel like you do not know them yet, so you may try to make up your own reasoning why you don't understand. Whether you feel like you have all things pertaining to life and godliness or not doesn't make this scripture untrue. You get to raise your reality to scripture, not the other way around, regardless of what you "see" or feel.

Regarding the topic of healing, you may have given up, settled into, or are afraid to pursue healing. No matter where you are in the process, I am praying for a new and fresh revelation of who God is for you. More importantly, I'm praying you will see His love for you. You have full permission to go with courage and confidence before the Father, knowing together you two will work out whatever in you needs attention. Since living in health means addressing all the areas of our lives, particularly our thought life, we will tackle a broad range of issues throughout this book.

As you continue to read, let this be your reminder: God wants you well and is not causing all the bad things in your life because He wants you to learn something. However, in your healing journey through this book, you will learn healing is available for you and offered freely. I pray this breeds new hope in your heart and in your body.

Never Alone

"Tomorrow I will stand on the top of the hill with the rod of God in my hand," Moses said in Exodus 17:9. Joshua did as Moses had commanded him to do: choose men and fight Amalek. Moses did as he promised: he went up the hill and held the rod of God in the air so Israel would prevail.

Hands up meant Israel prevailed. Hands down meant Amalek prevailed.

The problem with this story is Moses was still human, with human strength. Therefore, his arms began to feel heavy. Moses had physical limits. Verse 12 tells us, "Moses' hands became heavy; so they [Hur and Aaron] took a stone and put it under him, and he sat on it." Knowing what was at stake in the fight against Amalek, Hur and Aaron didn't stand on the sidelines. They went right into the battle together.

Aaron and Hur didn't stop with moving the rock. They also supported Moses' hands. One was on one side, and the other on the other side, which helped Moses keep his hands steady until the sun went down.

The end result? Joshua defeated Amalek. Top takeaway? Stop trying to do this alone.

This story with Aaron, Moses, and Hur encourages and reminds me I don't have to do the work alone, even when I feel alone. Sometimes I have to ask for help, and other times I must receive the help being offered. Asking for help isn't something I am always great at doing. I spent most of my life being independent. I cringed at the thought of someone else having to "carry" my burdens. I don't want someone to think less of me because of my weaknesses.

Two battles were going on at the same time in our story from Exodus. One battle was happening with Joshua and Amalek. The other battle was between Moses and his own physical strength. Imagine what this story would look like if Moses refused help and let his pride and ego get in the way. I don't know if Joshua would have defeated Amalek without Aaron and Hur helping Moses.

This is how I feel as I am writing this book. You are holding up your hands, and I am here to come alongside to say, "Keep going. I'm here to help." Your hands may start to feel heavy and like the battle is too strong for you to defeat. That's when the sweet reminder comes how your strength alone is not enough. Together we will do what Aaron and Hur did for Moses.

Second Corinthians 12:9 says, "'My grace is sufficient for you, for my power is made perfect in weakness.' Therefore I will boast all the more gladly about my weaknesses, so that Christ's power may rest on me" (NIV). Every one of us has weaknesses and strengths. In our weakness, we get to see God's strength in a powerful way. Today is a good day to surrender the lie that healing alone is the best way. Today is a good day to abandon the lie that your life will always be this way.

Pray this with me: *Father, forgive us for the times we try to do anything in our strength. We are weak without You. Give us a fresh revelation of Your strength today! In Your name, amen!*

Your body and soul are seen because a good Father dwells inside your good body. Now is the perfect time to begin to believe this truth.

CHAPTER / ONE

Creating Space for Healing

What do you do when you feel like you don't belong? Where do you go when you feel like you don't have a home?

Whenever my tears fell like rain, I ran into my closet and put my hands on my ears. I still heard the loud muffled sounds of screaming and yelling, as if thunder and lightning were rolling through on a dark and dreary night.

To cry was an echo of my present reality, one filled with heartache and despair.

In the other room was fighting (emotional and physical).

Words flew, but so did hands. The sounds still reached me of plates smashing against the wall, someone being thrown to the ground, or the front door slamming shut.

I grew up in a trailer park until I was in the third grade. You could smell the kerosene filling the small rooms, and the floorboards showed through because no carpet was present.

At a very young age, my brother and I sought adventures and outlets to deal with our reality. My brother took the route of alcohol and drugs to calm the rage inside, while I looked to men to experience moments of safety and love.

When you are young, you don't know you are in moments of survival. You don't know you are trying to find comfort. What you know is simple: How can I escape the present reality I am in? How can I get away from the yelling? The confusion? The pain?

The first time I gave my body to a man, I was twelve. At that age I had no clue the significance my body held or the story that God wanted to write (because I didn't know Him then).

In our pain, we do things that can easily fill us with regret, and then shame and guilt pour out. The shame and guilt continue to pour over, trying to fill a longing and belonging. I carried the shame and guilt side by side with sadness and anger.

They were not only my weapons; they were my safety net. If you got close enough to hurt me, you would experience my anger.

I was an average student in high school who was never disciplined enough to do her homework, but if anyone had been paying close attention, they would have seen my fight to live a different life than the generation before me. They would have seen a girl who tried to go to college twice and felt like a failure for not getting a degree.

Most importantly they would have seen a girl fighting for her life—to stay alive and survive. Therefore, she filled every moment she could with work or boyfriends, anything to keep her pain at bay and her body climbing the success ladder.

There was no space or time in my life to heal or to feel. Both of those things meant I had to face everything I was trying to run from.

Correcting Satan's Lies

Most of the things in my life felt steamrolled or as if I were pushing a ball of cement up a mountainside. I lived in a world where I felt unseen and as though I didn't matter, while simultaneously I tried to be the person others wanted me to be. I always believed, like most people do, that whatever happens to us has a purpose. Therefore, everything good or bad must have happened for a reason. Romans 8:28 says God will work all things together for our good. But when we fail to realize God doesn't cause the bad things to happen, we end up believing things outside of His character and nature.

He can use bad things and create good outcomes, yes. However, this doesn't mean He is causing all the bad things in our lives to happen so you and I can learn our lessons. God isn't a punisher.

I was like a broken-down car on the side of the road, missing some pieces and waiting for anyone to come along and fix me. It wasn't until many years later that I heard the words I needed to hear: "God's Word is a prescription for our health." I heard those words one night at Bible study. I felt like a little girl running up to her daddy so he could kiss her boo-boo—a little girl who knows she can trust her daddy. I discovered I had a Daddy in heaven who wanted to take my pain away. For the first time, God was someone I could trust. Coming to this realization set me on a journey to healing in which I had real hope that I would one day feel like myself again (whatever that felt like), that fear wouldn't always rule my heart.

What would happen if that's how we looked at the Father? Despite the pain we feel, what if we knew God was the Healer, we could trust Him, and He was a safe place for us to land?

Our hearts need a Father who cares for us. He is not a Father who is waiting for us to mess up so He can strike us for a sin we have committed. There are reasons things happen, but not everything happens for a reason. He's not sending us pain or sickness. We experience those things because of the sin in this world from the fall of Adam and Eve. There's a beautiful tension we're called to in this world: living with peace and joy even as we experience suffering, pain, and heartbreak. But how do we find peace and joy? God is the antidote and prescription for our pain. One of my favorite scriptures to remind me of this truth is from the book of Psalms.

> Bless the LORD, O my soul;
> And all that is within me, bless His holy name!
> Bless the LORD, O my soul,
> And forget not all His benefits:
> Who forgives all your iniquities,
> Who heals all your diseases,
> Who redeems your life from destruction,
> Who crowns you with lovingkindness and tender mercies,
> Who satisfies your mouth with good things,
> So that your youth is renewed like the eagle's. (103:1–5)

The psalmist reminds us of all His benefits. His promise to us is He will get us through the hard times and the results of sin because His Son paid for our sins.

The advice "refuse to settle for less than God's best"

challenged me in more ways than one. I had to decide if I would trust God with everything I was dealing with: heartbreak, fear, and worry. Could I trust that He had my back? That He would take care of me? Trusting God challenged me. As a child and teenager, I had to take care of myself because I felt like no one else would. The lie that no one would take care of me ran deep into my bones, like the roots of a fifty-year-old tree. Would I allow God to step in and tend to my needs like no one ever had?

Something important I had to grasp and take more seriously than before was that a real enemy is at work. Here are some attributes of the enemy to be aware of:

- He's the accuser.

> Now there was a day when the sons of God (angels) came to present themselves before the LORD, and Satan (adversary, accuser) also came among them. (Job 1:6 AMP)

- He portrays himself as the angel of light.

> For Satan himself transforms himself into an angel of light. (2 Corinthians 11:14)

- He is our adversary.

> Be sober, be vigilant; because your adversary the devil walks about like a roaring lion, seeking whom he may devour. (1 Peter 5:8)

Knowing some of the characteristics of the accuser, we realize he targets us, trying any way he can to drive a wedge between God and us. He'll use lies, misconceptions, and our own concepts of "normal" to lead us off track. Of course, our focus shouldn't be on the enemy, but we are responsible for knowing what weapons he tries to use against us, knowing who he can use against us, and understanding his nature. Often, I see the enemy portraying himself as one of God's angels of light. He twists the truth and then, once again, whispers lies that blame God for all the destruction in our lives.

Here's what I know now and what I discuss as we move through this book together: God is the Healer. He's not into pain management. He's a pain taker. We have gone through situations in the past that have kept us from experiencing God to the fullest. Maybe someone told you God was angry with you about your past. Maye someone in your life continues to speak words that make you feel inadequate. Perhaps you were told God keeps giving you lessons to learn from, which causes you to keep your heavenly Father at arm's length.

Whatever continues to keep you from experiencing God to the fullest, I'm here to walk with you and to help you process through some of those things that I had to overcome as well.

Father, let the veil lift from our eyes.

Set Up the Space

Setting up space for healing—receiving what Jesus did on the cross for us—will be the less visible miracle with the most significant impact . . . if we give time and space to heal. To create space is to set aside time in our day, allowing us to slow down, even for a minute, to think about what we are thinking. Much of our healing will be partnering with God, whom we cannot see but can experience. Partnering with God will heal wounded places that are not visible to the naked eye but that the soul can feel.

When we are healing from lies, one of the first steps is to write down the thoughts we think on a regular basis. What stories show up repeatedly throughout our day or in specific events? If we do not know what we believe, then the gap from the spiritual to the physical will get wider, causing us to feel distant from our bodies and distant from God. Day to day, I fight back the narrative in my head that says I am not doing enough. I try to fill my to-do list with enough tasks so I can feel like a success. If I do not put that way of thinking into submission with truth, I end the day with an exhausted body and an overwhelmed mind. Every day I remind myself His grace is sufficient for me and He causes the increase, not me. Now is the time to ask: What narratives do I tell myself throughout the day?

Once we begin to recognize the stories—the narratives—we tell ourselves, the second step is to name them and write them down. If they are phrases, think of the feeling you experience with those phrases. Naming our feelings helps us begin to move through them with clarity and effectiveness. We no longer guess what we feel; we are aware of what we feel. Even though not naming them may feel safer, masking our feelings can make them difficult to regulate and bring into submission to God's Word.

After we spend time naming them, our third step is to create the time to spend with God to read His Word and know what He has to say about what we feel. His Word trumps anything we feel. We can believe God even when we don't experience His love wrapping around our feelings in the moment.

These three steps will bring awareness and help us move in the direction of healing with God's Word because the gospel message heals the soul and brings life into our bodies. The hard and holy work is not the physical act but the spiritual discipline that causes us to act—recognizing what we believe will affect how we see.

One of my favorite ways to create space is to get outside, go for a walk, and be in nature. Therefore, I start the process by moving my body and walking with God through what I am experiencing. After I allow myself to process internally through the day, I grab the notebook I keep next to my bed at night. I dump out everything I was feeling for the day into my notebook to see what I was thinking on paper—to name every feeling and emotion. Then I can begin to make sense of what was causing me to feel turmoil and uneasiness in my body. Renewing our minds will take time. Working through past experiences and trauma will require patience. Learning why we respond and react the way we do will take consistency. Every time we create space for healing, we make more room in our hearts to know God on a deeper, more intimate level.

Why We Need Space

We try to create space in our lives with planners, diets, or routines, but the truth is that these tools are the last thing we need. The depth of our soul is like diving miles deep into the ocean without ever seeing the bottom floor. Our soul carries us through this life while holding our beliefs, pain, and experiences.

Adding stickers to a planner, trying to find the perfect diet to make us feel better, or creating one more habit is like putting ointment on top of a bandage. Adding one more task or item doesn't address or heal the real issue. Trying to work out our healing with skin-deep tasks avoids and covers the wound. Creating space for healing allows us not to worry about doing more but to rest in who God is so we can learn about who we are. We are made in His likeness. To know God is to know ourselves (as we discuss later in the book).

You know you need space if thinking about doing one more thing feels like adding twenty-pound bricks to an already heavy load. Pretty soon, the load feels like too much to carry. Maybe you realize you have lost your peace and joy, and you no longer laugh, let alone have fun. When was the last time you laughed so hard your stomach hurt, or you had peace even though it felt like a tornado was passing through your life?

What we want most is to feel seen, known, heard, safe, and loved. Our soul runs deep like the ocean because our Father goes deep with us. He's not superficial. God isn't treading water, hoping we survive. He's in the water with us, telling us we can handle what comes against us, and there is more to life than the hustle. God is not looking at how much we do or how great our body is. He wants to know if He has our attention—all our attention.

The Kind of Space We Need

Healing is what we want most: to be seen, known, heard, safe, and loved. But it can often become one of the hardest things for us to find time to do. We want to have healing without making the investment of time, patience, faith, and the constant pursuit of what the Father says, despite what we feel.

Moving from what we feel to trusting God's Word is not easy. You'll often feel a tug-of-war within you, with God's Word on one side and the enemy's lies on the other. Living from God's Word is not easy because we often live through our tangible, physical reality and everything we experience through our senses. When we get to the point where what we put off or shove under the rug hits us headfirst in our day-to-day actions, then what do we do?

What I realized about healing is that real change happens through internal spiritual change. We often ask: What will healing my soul bring to my physical reality? How will healing benefit me in my life? We then decide if healing is worth the time. But why wait to hit rock bottom before we pursue the answers our soul needs?

Not much is required of us to be focused on the external,

so we put our efforts there and downplay the impact and power of healing internally. But when we take care of our souls, even though we can't "see" healing, we can feel it. Let's look at the story of the paralytic man found in Luke 5:18–24:

> Men brought on a bed a man who was paralyzed, whom they sought to bring in and lay before Him. And when they could not find how they might bring him in, because of the crowd, they went up on the housetop and let him down with his bed through the tiling into the midst before Jesus. When He saw their faith, He said to him, "Man, your sins are forgiven you." And the scribes and the Pharisees began to reason, saying, "Who is this who speaks blasphemies? Who can forgive sins but God alone?"
>
> But when Jesus perceived their thoughts, He answered and said to them, "Why are you reasoning in your hearts? Which is easier, to say, 'Your sins are forgiven you,' or to say, 'Rise up and walk'? But that you may know that the Son of Man has power on earth to forgive sins"—He said to the man who was paralyzed, "I say to you, arise, take up your bed, and go to your house."

In this passage, we see friends helping their paralytic friend down through a roof so he could encounter Jesus and receive healing. The Pharisees and scribes chime in and try to reason what they see when Jesus, in essence, asks them what is easier, to say our sins are forgiven or to have physical healing? Physical healing appears to be harder because healing physically would require a miraculous act, something our eyes could see. However, the Pharisees seem to think forgiveness doesn't have any value to add to our physical world. They want evidence or proof the healing happened.

What they don't seem to understand is God works from

the spiritual to the external. We often try to work from the external to the spiritual. The proof is what our hearts desire before believing becomes a reality. God wants us to believe Him before we ever see our prayers come to life. Chasing the outcome—the desired result—is easy without addressing what can bring the desired result. He shows us in this passage the importance of who He is and what He came to do. The less-visible miracle is Jesus came to forgive our sins, which is the miracle that should be getting our attention the most.

Through the story of the paralytic man and the questions the Pharisees and scribes asked, we see a gap between the spiritual and physical. The gap is our belief or our unbelief. The kind of space we need to heal our souls requires us to close the gap between the spiritual and physical (the internal and the external). This will require unraveling the lies that carry our unbelief. When we unravel the lies, we can step into the truth, belief, and how God has always been there for us. Ironically, we need space to close the gap. Slowing down long enough, taking time out of our day, and knowing what we believe will be crucial to closing the gap.

CHAPTER / TWO

The Identity Effect

One day I made three promises to myself that would shape how I lived my life for many years. Sarah, someone close to me at the time, was driving me to work.

I was about sixteen, looking out the window watching the trees and houses go by fast enough that they became nothing but a faded background. My mind was full of thoughts racing by as I listened to Sarah's usual topic of choice: how miserable, worn out, and poor she was. As I listened, my thoughts began to form together like pieces from a puzzle. When they all found their proper positions,

I made the three promises to myself. I said, "Jess, you will always have food, you will always have water, and you will always have heat." Those promises may seem strange to some, but for me, they were not a given. When I was growing up, my parents took care of us (my brother and me) the best way they knew how. However, that left us multiple times without much food besides bread for toast, with no hot water, and with no heat to stay warm. Sometimes I would have only one of these, all of them, or none. My hair often got washed in the sink with water so cold it felt as if icicles were forming in my hair. Curled up under the blankets on my bed is where you would often find me, because my bed was the warmest place in the house, thanks to my little space heater. Cooking on electric pans became normal when there was no gas to turn on the stove.

The moment I made those three commitments to myself was when I knew I would never give up or give in to any future tough times. Working hard, long, and in as many jobs as possible was how I would prove to others that I could live a different life than I experienced early on. Those promises formed deep roots in my soul at such a young age. They became what drove my need to hustle later in life, leading me to extreme burnout and exhaustion. I got lost in my work and didn't know who I was. A simple question such as "Jess, what do you like to do for fun?" left me speechless, because fun wasn't something to be had when you had to grow up fast and keep the promises you made to your sixteen-year-old self.

My family of origin is not to blame. How I was raised doesn't limit who I can become in the Lord today. We are all messy people who bring past pain into current and future relationships. As you will continue to learn throughout this book, the stories you tell yourself about specific events in your life will impact how you show up in every other area of your life.

Sinking Ship

I promised myself a life without starvation, extreme cold, or homelessness. Have you made promises to yourself that you are striving to keep hold of with a firm grip?

"I won't be the parent my parents were to me."

"I must have the best job to prove to people I can do what they always said I couldn't do."

"My kids will always have what I didn't have."

"I'll never let someone hurt me again."

These promises we make keep a wall up and build a fortress around our pain. The promises (masked as truth but actually lies) become gasoline to our burning insecurities. At first, the fire might keep us warm. But the blaze becomes impossible to control and feels unbearable to put out.

To slow the fire in any area of our lives, we tend to go along with this idea that "finding balance" in our lives will cause the fire to suffocate, and things will feel "normal." We suspect that if we have control and order in our lives, we will feel as though we have power over our circumstances too. If we could figure out a way to get everything to feel equal, in place, then life itself wouldn't feel so chaotic. But external balance doesn't take care of the hole in our souls. Our goal in this book isn't finding balance; it has more to do with soul searching within Scripture.

To start our soul search, many people suggest learning about the different areas of life we should focus on, to figure out which area needs (or areas need) more attention. A few categories are finances, relationships, personal growth, and spiritual growth. We could rate our happiness in each category and mark the categories we want to improve. We could then create a plan to increase those areas. However, focusing only on these specific portions of our lives while ignoring the pain and feelings we may have around them is like organizing the cargo of a sinking ship.

Instead of working to improve each area, what if we first take a step back and plug the hole in our souls? We can do this by dealing with what's behind the physical actions and lack of contentment and real identity. We've already talked about how God deals with emotional/spiritual issues before delving into the physical. And He wants us to do the same. What God knows is the emotional part of us tends to get ignored, which is why areas of our lives will feel out of balance. Ignoring our emotional side sets off a chain reaction that leads to our lives being out of balance; we topple and punch holes in our life's ship. Our desire to be everything to everyone and to do anything and everything has left us with worn-out bodies and holes in our weary souls.

Here are five emotional responses that tend to knock us out of balance and keep us from going deeper in our healing:

1. People pleasing
2. Guilt and obligation
3. Misplaced identity
4. No boundaries
5. Emptiness

People Pleasing

People pleasing is our inability to say no. No matter how much we want to say no, yes still comes out of our mouths. Those tend to be the moments we say yes and feel immediate regret afterward. The more we say yes when we feel we should say no, we set ourselves up for one area of our lives (or multiple areas) to begin to feel out of balance or out of control. The area we keep saying yes to becomes a place we dread or a place of exhaustion. For example, maybe we say too many yeses for work projects or too many yeses to exercise when we should rest. I always know when I am people pleasing when the work that comes with my yes feels heavy and forced, and a sense of dread comes upon me. I start to come up with excuses and scenarios in my head about how I can get out of the thing I just said yes to.

We can overcommit in any area of our lives. We have this desire for balance, but the need to please rules our hearts.

> For am I now seeking the approval of man, or of God? Or am I trying to please man? If I were still trying to please man, I would not be a servant of Christ. (Galatians 1:10 ESV)

Paul knew people would disagree with him. But he wasn't willing to water down the message to please the people in front of him. He didn't need the approval of man, because he knew he was found in Christ.

Unfortunately, not everyone has this strength. John 12:43 tells us about people who "loved the approval of men more than the approval of God" (AMP). These people believed in Jesus, but because of the Pharisees, they did not confess Him publicly. If they did, they would lose the ability to go into the synagogue.

Guilt and Obligation

Guilt and obligation make saying no harder. We feel the need to repay people even if repayment is unnecessary, not asked for, and not required. Sometimes receiving is hard because we don't think we are worth what others do for us. Or maybe we don't trust the giver. I learned at a young age that when someone did something nice for me, they kept what they did locked in a memory bank to use later when they needed something. I have spent a lot of time learning to receive with a thankful heart, without feeling the need to make up for the gift given.

Or maybe you feel guilt and obligation in the area of comparison. You make homemade cookies because your child's classmate's mom made homemade cookies. Even though you hate baking, and your child isn't asking you to make homemade cookies and would love you regardless, the guilt of not being a baker like other moms begins to reign in your heart. Sometimes our hearts crave the idea of having our lives put together with a pretty red bow. The pretty red bow helps us fit into the mirage of appearing as if we have our lives together like everyone else we see in this social-media-focused world. We exchange delight for duty. Although we want balance, guilt and obligation rule our hearts.

Misplaced Identity

Misplaced identity is when our job, body, status, or bank account becomes the measure of who we are. We focus on our work or our weight instead of the God of grace. We find ourselves putting all of who we are into this one specific area (or multiple areas) of our lives.

This means when an area is not doing so well, neither are we. Riding the waves of our emotions becomes our way of life. When our identity becomes misplaced, we are lost at sea and the areas of our life begin to feel scattered, like wreckage from a ship. We scramble to keep all the pieces of our misplaced identity together, but our emotional attachment to them means the fullness of who God made us sinks beneath the waves—meaning, if we allow physical/external things to define us, we have to make sure those areas are doing well even if we are slowly becoming more and more exhausted trying to swim while holding it all up.

I allowed men to tell me what love is, my body to tell

me how much I am worth, and people's opinions to form my future. My misplaced identity, for example, looked like working out at the gym to the point of burnout and exhaustion so I could hopefully have a body that got me the attention I thought I needed to prove I was seen. I held God at arm's length and searched for my identity in everything but Him. Exodus 20:3 makes whom we should worship clear. God commands nothing should become an idol in our lives, saying, "You shall have no other gods before Me." This scripture reminds us only He can fully sustain us.

No Boundaries

We may allow things to happen or people to speak to us in an unhealthy way rather than creating a healthy space between the situation or person. There are a lot of boundaries and layers to boundaries. Learning your limits may require a counselor or coach to establish what boundaries are and what they look like in everyday life. However, not taking the time to understand or learn about boundaries may lead other people to dictate or rule our lives and choices. Boundaries keep us feeling safe, seen, protected, and respected. They allow us to begin to have a healthier relationship with people we come into contact with, our work, and anything that can trigger us.

Boundaries can be emotional, physical, and even digital. For example, we can have boundaries with our cell phones and allot specific times to scroll through social media. Setting specific times can help protect our joy. We can also have physical boundaries in dating. Trust me, I know boundaries can feel hard because sometimes saying nothing feels easier than saying something. The depth of our pain can determine our limits. The more we step into healing, the more we will be able to reinforce the boundaries.

The first boundary I set was with Bill, a distant relative. Bill is known for his anger issues, which I have experienced many times. Before engaging in a conversation with Bill, I had to be clear on the expectation of our conversation. The boundary was set when I told him he would need to stay calm in our conversation or I would leave our conversation until he could speak to me with respect and kindness. Moments later, after discussing my expectations, the cuss words came flying at the same time my finger touched the end-call button.

Boundaries are not easy, but they create a line to protect you and the other party (or parties) from going farther than either of you are comfortable with.

Emptiness

Sometimes it feels as if life wrings us out. There is nothing left to give and so we hang ourselves out to dry. Suddenly we don't know how we feel, what to feel, or what to think. Therefore, we reach for anything to feel again. We end up disconnected from our bodies and brains. Will someone or something come along to nurture the parts that feel rough and dry? We do not know what brings us joy or fills us up, so we hope physical balance restores and refills the areas where emptiness has settled in. We want balance, but the holes in our hearts are crying for attention.

I'll never forget the moment the Lord showed me how much my heart was crying for attention. I was on my way to the gym—the gym I went to at least five days a week, for two hours at a time sometimes—to meet with my trainer. I was getting warmed up with a weight I had lifted before doing a back squat. As I was coming up from the back squat with my trainer standing there, my hips shifted, and I felt as if my hips or lower back gave out. In a matter of seconds, I was in physical pain. The pain was like a thousand bolts of electricity shooting through my pelvis and down my legs. The burning pain sent tears streaming down my face like racing horses. My pain soon turned into numbness and with every step I feared failure. Failure of my muscles, failure of my mind and body connection, but most of all, fear that I was derailed from my goals. In those moments, when I didn't know when I would be able to work out again, the Lord whispered to my broken soul, "You have put every ounce of your existence into what your body looks like." I wanted my body to be the area that smoothed out the rough places in my life.

Neglecting the parts of us trying to communicate something deeper can leave us reaching for a life of balance at every corner, which is why balance doesn't exist. Assuming there is balance is to assume every area of our life is of equal importance, or we are giving our attention equally to all. If we want to assume balance from a place where our priorities are in check and honored, that's important. However, when our life feels out of balance and we try to "do better" without "knowing better," it can hurt more than help us. When we notice we're struggling with these emotional areas—people pleasing, guilt and obligation, misplaced identity, a lack of boundaries, and emptiness—it's a signal to look deeper to discover our real and true identity.

Addressing the Biggest Need

The promises I made to myself at age sixteen not only showed my inability to allow God to love me but also revealed my incorrect view of who the Father is—who I thought He was and what I thought His response would be regarding the choices I made (or would make). I felt like our relationship had become a dangerous road to tread. The fear of making the wrong choices. The worry of saying the right thing and having to know everything. The reality was that I viewed God through the lens of my relationship experiences here on earth more often than not. How others treated me on earth was what I thought I would also get from my heavenly Father. How could I trust or feel safe with a heavenly Father, when I felt so let down, hurt, and misunderstood by people in this world?

The most tender place we can heal is our soul, which can impact our identity and worth. Like a captain of a ship who is in command and responsible for the safety of his crew, God is the master commander of our lives who we can trust to guide us to safety in rocky waters. God is the key to fixing the leaks in our tender souls. Understanding our identity doesn't happen because of a feeling but because of a Person. Knowing this can create a safe place for our emotions to land.

Our identity, how we see the Father, and how we see ourselves affect how we live and show up in this world. God is a constant Father who never leaves us in a place of lack, wants to tend to our needs, and doesn't leave us feeling guilt, shame, or condemnation.

Here are three questions we can consider about our identity to take us deeper into a relationship with Christ.

1. What's causing you to go under and punching holes in your identity?

Is all of who you are becoming wrapped up in one thing? Are pieces of who you are put into compartments of your life to keep you feeling as though you have everything all together and in control? We become what we focus on most. Knowing where our identity comes from is one thing. Yet knowing we are loved, seen, and cared for by our Father in heaven is living from a different place—a heavenly place. Knowing we are loved is simple, but living loved is not easy. Therefore, when we allow ourselves to zoom in on those areas where we are setting our gaze, which have become our places of security other than Jesus, we can begin rebuilding a solid foundation in Him. For example, looking at my work through a magnifying glass allowed me to see the extra layers of meaning around working hard.

Working hard wasn't bad until I made working hard my idol, which turned to hustle. Taking a closer look at my worth ethic allowed me to take a moment to understand my actions versus living from a place of emotion. To zoom in is to take a closer look, to know our worth and identity in Christ come from a place of rest, not from a place of working to feel deserving of rest. We are still children of God, whether we feel worthy or not, because being worthy has nothing to do with what we can do and everything to do with what He has done.

I have had more hustle days than rest days. Days where I would try to use my work to prove how worthy I was. I can still remember the moments at the end of a workday, throughout my twenties, when all I wanted to do was grab all my soft, comfortable blankets and head up to bed. I wanted to close my eyes and drift off to sleep because I didn't feel like anything I did that day was of importance or value, which in return made me feel as though I was not of importance or of value either. Spend the time to go to the places where you feel like you don't have significance with Him—knowing you don't have to heal alone—so your value will not become wrapped up in your works or feelings but in the One who saved you from yourself.

A hard truth is many of us are trying to figure out who we are without ever opening our Bibles. At times, following people who have the same beliefs as we have feels easier than opening our Bibles.

Doing this doesn't challenge us to higher or deeper thinking. We get caught up in the feel-good messages that confirm everything we feel, which leads us into the deep water of the false ideal of balance. Then there are messages that feel good for the sake of not wanting to challenge us but rather feed our ego and our self-righteousness to prove a point. Some biblical messages are hard for us to hear because we haven't reached a specific level of revelation and renewing yet. Learning about the nature of God doesn't come tied to another person's opinion. We get to sit with God for ourselves as we ask the Holy Spirit to reveal the words we read.

2. What storms have changed your view of God?

Who you believe God to be will impact who you think you are. Genesis 1:27 tells us, "God created man in His own image; in the image of God He created him; male and female He created them." Let's break down "His own image" from the passage. According to Google dictionary, the definition of *image* is "a person or thing that closely resembles another." Similar words would be *likeness, replica, look-alike,* and *copy.* You and I are the ultimate image-bearers of God. The repetition of God saying He created us is also a sweet reminder that our identity should be in no one else but Him. We were His good idea from the beginning.

Here is how we can know that we are a good idea. Ephesians 1:5 says we were chosen "according to the good pleasure of His will." Through "the good pleasure of His will," we become adopted sons and daughters. We are wanted and accepted by our Father. Verse 6 says, "To the praise of the glory of His grace, by which He made us accepted in the Beloved." According to Merriam-Webster, *accepted* means "regarded favorably, given approval or acceptance." The Lord is not tolerating us. He didn't create us in His image to leave us hopeless, in lack, or as a victim. Our Father loves us—head over heels, to the moon and back, more than the sand grains on the seashore, without-limits kind of love. His love is deeper than the ocean and extends beyond the clouds in the sky. Zephaniah 3:17 reminds us God rejoices over us: "The LORD your God is in your midst, a Warrior who saves. He will rejoice over you with joy; He will be quiet in His love [making no mention of your past sins], He will rejoice over you with shouts of joy" (AMP).

What does this have to do with our identities? Everything. If we don't view our Father through the lens of love, then how we view ourselves will not be through the lens of love either. We are made in His likeness—in His image. So, the image we see in Him will be the image we see in us. This is why the importance of knowing who we believe Him to be matters.

3. Do you know the God who calms the sea? Do you know God's true character and nature?

We see Him in the Old Testament. However, knowing God in the New Testament under a new covenant is crucial. We are born into a new covenant because God sent His Son, Jesus, to die in our place. Through Jesus, our new covenant allows us to have direct communication and intimacy with God, which we didn't have in the old covenant. The only way to learn about who He is, is to read His Word.

- God is light.

  > This is the message which we have heard from Him and declare to you, that God is light and in Him is no darkness at all. (1 John 1:5)

- God is patient.

> The Lord is not slack concerning His promise, as some count slackness, but is longsuffering toward us, not willing that any should perish but that all should come to repentance. (2 Peter 3:9)

- God gives.

> For God so loved the world that he gave his one and only Son, that whoever believes in him shall not perish but have eternal life. (John 3:16 NIV)

We need to be able to see the true commander of our lives for who He truly is and not through the lens of our pain or our past.

Ask Him to reveal Himself before we turn to anyone else to help us identify God's true nature.

Repairing Our Shipwrecked Souls

I love how Romans 12:9–21 reveals to us what God's heart is for, and He calls us into action. The heading for this passage in the NKJV is "Behave Like a Christian." After we answer the three questions about our identity, we have to begin to move toward the truth we know. A ship can only begin to repair when it's in its harbor and no longer sinking. Repairing our shipwrecked soul will involve us taking each individual passage we read in the Word of God and welding those words into the holes in our soul. No longer will we continue to plug the holes only for a force to come through and unplug them. We no longer have to merely survive through our pain and suffering. He comes to guide and help us through our pain and suffering. God's Word seals the deal and begins to weld the holes shut.

> Let love be without hypocrisy. Abhor what is evil. Cling to what is good. Be kindly affectionate to one another with brotherly love, in honor giving preference to one another;

not lagging in diligence, fervent in spirit, serving the Lord; rejoicing in hope, patient in tribulation, continuing steadfastly in prayer; distributing to the needs of the saints, given to hospitality.
Bless those who persecute you; bless and do not curse. Rejoice with those who rejoice, and weep with those who weep. Be of the same mind toward one another. Do not set your mind on high things, but associate with the humble. Do not be wise in your own opinion.
Repay no one evil for evil. Have regard for good things in the sight of all men. If it is possible, as much as depends on you, live peaceably with all men. Beloved, do not avenge yourselves, but rather give place to wrath; for it is written, "Vengeance is Mine, I will repay," says the Lord. Therefore "If your enemy is hungry, feed him; If he is thirsty, give him a drink; For in so doing you will heap coals of fire on his head." Do not be overcome by evil, but overcome evil with good. (Romans 12:9–21)

Almost every sentence in this passage has one or more behavior traits for us to meditate on. How do I handle those who persecute me? How do I handle the evil that comes my way? When times are tough, what am I called to do?

Romans 12:9–21 is a beautiful example of God's love for us and for others. He's always moving us in the direction of His love, and His love transforms our hearts. Every time we move in the direction of truth, a hole gets welded closed. Everything about this passage is contrary to how the world would tell us to respond. When we are living contrary to the world, we know God is leading us, not ourselves. He calls us higher; He calls us to heal.

———•✦✦✦✦•———

Remember that what's causing you to go under and punching holes in your identity, the storms that have changed your view of God, and knowing the God who calms the sea all impact how we view the world.

Knowing the answers to these questions can impact who we believe we are, because we were made in the Father's image.

Take the time to go through each section in this chapter again. Answer the questions honestly and then go to His Word to see if what you "feel" is, in fact, true to what is real (according to Scripture). Be willing to think about where you may have formed beliefs that don't line up with Scripture. Are they your beliefs or beliefs you adapted and inherited from those who have been around you most of your life? Getting caught up in everyday life is easy. Slowing down long enough to challenge the way you think is harder. Today is the day you give yourself permission to slow down and do so.

CHAPTER / THREE

Discerning the Truth

I picked up the same size pants I'd worn for years off the clothes rack. This particular day was a cold winter day, the kind when I leave the house wearing layers of clothes, with five-day-old messy hair in a bun under my beanie and boots to complete the ensemble. I took the pants and headed to the dressing room. My head was spinning as usual. How would those few square feet of privacy make me feel this time? Pants are either my best friend or my enemy. The mirror either boosted my confidence or stole it within a second. I begrudgingly found the largest stall at the end of the fitting room and took a deep breath as I unclipped the jeans from the hanger. As I began to put one leg in followed by the other, I started to do the dance—you know the dance.

The dance says, "These are tighter than I thought they would be."

When the pants stopped midthigh, all the thoughts began to come for me:

How did I get here?

Did I let my body go?

I have worn this size for years. What happened?

I have not bought this brand in a while. Maybe the manufacturer changed how the pants are made?

Maybe this style doesn't run true to size? Did I get lazy?

I took another look in the mirror, gathered my things, and came to these conclusions:

My legs are different.

My body is different. I'm up a size.

What does buying a size up in pants mean about me?

My first reaction was to go hard-core: cut everything I was eating that was not healthy and get to working out. I believed nothing I was doing up to that point was working. Trying on those pants put my thoughts into a state of turmoil. I felt confused, not knowing what to believe about the bigger pants, and disturbed to find out how much my thighs grew. Then I came to another conclusion: Buying the bigger size wasn't what concerned me the most. What mattered the most was what I thought those pants meant about me.

I began to believe the lie that I was lazy. Then I stopped and dug a little deeper. To continue to believe this lie would validate my feelings as though they were true. Believing the lie that I was lazy was fuel to my feelings of frustration because I tend to ride the pendulum from the side of freedom to the side of restriction when it comes to food and working out. I learned the more we validate our feelings, the more they compound.

That leads me to this question: Have you ever heard the same phrase over and over again—so much so that you can no longer remember where the phrase came from or whether what was said was true or merely an opinion? Maybe someone close to you called you lazy or boring or ugly or mean, and years later you find showing up to real life is hard, and you revisit the time someone spoke those words over you.

No matter the phrase or words someone uses to speak over us, if someone tells a lie to us or about us long enough, we begin to believe it is true. The words we meditate on will be the words we reproduce. Anything in repetition builds something. We may be creating stories about ourselves based on other people's pain and how they view their lives and world. Think of us as sponges. Whatever substance a sponge is soaking in will come out when the sponge is wrung out. Our lives are similar. We absorb our surroundings, other people's pain, and our circumstances all at once. What we soak in will flow from our hearts and out of our mouths.

Now the question turns to us: What have we been soaking in? Opinions? Past moments? Trauma? Pain? Joy? The truth?

We can soak up both truth and lies into our lives. Lies

keep us trapped in stories that don't exist and are not real or based on truth.

The stories we believe based on lies not only keep us trapped and circling the same mountain, but the lies keep us from seeing the truth. Lies keep us from healing. Our past pain can guide our present reality, which can hardwire our brain to believe specific thoughts to be true that are more likely lies and attacks on our identity. Recognizing the lies is crucial to transforming the way we live and see the world around us. The awareness of God's Word brings attention to the lies. When we bring God's Word into our current thoughts, our thoughts are confronted with two opposing viewpoints. Since Jesus is the embodiment of truth, anything that goes against His Word is a lie.

We hardwire our brains when the same thoughts occur, and the way of living remains the same day in and day out. When our thinking begins to change—when we elevate our thinking to God's truth—we prune old neural pathways and form new ones. When we realize that Jesus invites us to see His perspective and not ours, then healing comes through His kindness and compassion extending toward our pain and experiences.

Healing has a welcome invitation when we grant permission to ourselves to bring up parts of us that are buried or to rest when needed. Processing through pain and forgiveness does not mean what you experienced does not exist or is not valid. We can experience our feelings and, at the same time, not allow them to form into our worth or our identity. After purchasing the bigger pants, I allowed myself to feel sad and angry. I didn't try to shove down the reality and truth about the size of the pants. I allowed myself to carry sadness so that I could experience wholeness. I was experiencing my feelings at the same time as training a new way of thinking (out of the lies) about my body and myself.

Holding both our feelings and God's truth is where we

begin to bridge the gap from feeling to healing. A good way to determine whether we believe a lie or not is by asking ourselves a few simple questions:

1. What kind of fruit is my life creating right now?
2. What do I think about most of the time?
3. How are my thoughts making me feel?

Asking these questions requires us to think about what we are thinking. The more of God's Word we have stored in our hearts, the easier detecting the lies will become. Awareness requires us to ask the Holy Spirit to help us be aware so that we can repair.

Know the Truth

As the Holy Spirit brings awareness, reading God's Word brings truth. Recognizing the lie requires you to know the truth. Without the truth, the lie has nothing to be compared with. We end up taking one event in our life and weighing the current event against it. Picture Peeta from *The Hunger Games*. By the time we get to the fourth movie, Peeta has endured a lot of emotional and physical trauma after being captured by the Capital. Katniss is sent out to create propos (propaganda) for the war, and the Capital brings Peeta, who is still unstable, to join the rest of the unit because of his outburst of rage and anger—a result of the trauma. Peeta no longer views Katniss as his ally but rather views her as both ally and enemy, depending on what triggers him. There is a moment when the sun is beginning to rise when Katniss is on duty to watch over Peeta. He begins to get verbally hostile with Katniss. Moments later, he makes a profound statement: "I don't know what is true anymore." Peeta's friend Finnick wakes up and responds with one simple answer: "Then ask."

Our past trauma and pain distort our present reality to the extent that we sometimes do not know what is real or true anymore. Finnick's response sends a reminder to us as well: Are we asking what is true?

Truth, by definition, is exclusive—meaning there cannot be two opposing truths simultaneously, or they cancel each other out. There can be more than one true event that happened in our lives. Yet, there is one truth (God's Word) who gets the final say over them (your pain and trauma).

Over time, the opinions become stacked on each other. Sooner or later, we begin to crumble at the pressures of life and want to retreat with a white flag of surrender, which says we aren't good enough.

Therefore, to know a lie is to know the fruit the lie produces in our lives. A lie will lead to destruction of some kind, whether defeat in our thought life, jealousy or insecurities in our relationships, or feeling stuck in our purpose or where God has called us. Lies lead us to stay in one place for an extended amount of time. Lies don't want to see us win. John 8:44 tells us that Satan is not only a liar, he's "the father of lies" (NIV). There is no truth in him.

The enemy is a liar. He wants to replace the truth in our hearts and souls with deception. If the enemy can keep us distracted and focused on our painful lies, he can keep us distant from God.

Focusing on Truth

Satan keeps us distant from God by placing seeds in our hands. Those seeds are thoughts. Those thoughts can keep growing the distance between who we are in Christ and who the world says we have to be if we water them.

Every thought we have (*I hate my body; I am so sick; I am no good*) is a seed we plant. What we plant, we harvest. Planting an apple seed will not produce an orange.

The thoughts we plant in the soil of our hearts grow, forming deep roots. Depending on the seed and the type of soil, we will grow weeds or flowers.

Many passages in Scripture refer to what to talk about, what to meditate on, how we should think, and why the way we think is important. For example, Philippians 4:8–9 teaches us what to focus on and what to do with what we are focusing on. But before we get to verses 8–9, read verses 6–7: "Be anxious for nothing, but in everything by prayer and supplication, with thanksgiving, let your requests be made known to God; and the peace of God, which surpasses all understanding, will guard your hearts and minds through Christ Jesus." His Word is a constant reminder, pointing us back to His strength in our weakness.

God knew from the beginning how our thought life was going to affect us. With our free will comes the ability to choose, and that means our thought life is a choice too. His love is good because He already equipped us with the tools we need.

While Philippians 4:6–7 gives us guidance on not being anxious about anything, and tells us that everything we do, we should bring before God who will guard us, verses 8–9 instruct us on what to think about:

> Finally, brethren, whatever things are true, whatever things are noble, whatever things are just, whatever things are pure, whatever things are lovely, whatever things are of good report, if there is any virtue and if there is anything praiseworthy—meditate on these things. The things which you learned and received and heard and saw in me, these do, and the God of peace will be with you.

Our thought life is essential for our emotional (and often our physical) health because every thought becomes a biochemical reaction. You will learn later how the brain will release specific signals to the body, where they act as messengers of the thought. When the signals are released, they create a matching set of reactions to align with what the brain is thinking. The signaling means there is a constant state of communication between the body and the brain. If we see our favorite sweet treat at the grocery store or a party, our stomach may begin to growl as our brain sends signals to our body that we are hungry and excited.

Therefore, opposing the lies will only come through growing our relationship with the Father. Our feelings are not a sin. Repeat: not a sin. How we handle our feelings is what matters to God. Luke 6:27–31 paints a beautiful picture about how to handle ourselves when others spew hate words in our faces, curse our goals and dreams, or mistreat us with their words or their hands:

> But to you who are listening I say: Love your enemies, do good to those who hate you, bless those who curse you, pray for those who mistreat you. If someone slaps you on one cheek, turn to them the other also. If someone takes your coat, do not withhold your shirt from them. Give to everyone who asks you, and if anyone takes what belongs to you, do not demand it back. Do to others as you would have them do to you. (NIV)

Luke 6:27–31 is not an example of how to get walked on like a doormat but how to begin to heal with the Lord and not allow our feelings to guide our lives.

His Word tells us we have the power to control our feelings and work through them without allowing them to escalate. We do not have to guess the results we get when we respond from our feelings. Without creating space, responding from pain or upset ends in more frustration, loss, anger, or hurt. To catch every thought and discern what is truth or a lie is not about perfection.

Here are a few scriptures to point us back to discernment, control, and letting the Holy Spirit do the work.

So then, my beloved brethren, let every man be swift to hear, slow to speak, slow to wrath; for the wrath of man does not produce the righteousness of God. (James 1:19–20)

He who is slow to anger has great understanding [and profits from his self-control], but he who is quick-tempered exposes and exalts his foolishness [for all to see]. (Proverbs 14:29 AMP)

"Be angry, and do not sin": do not let the sun go down on your wrath, nor give place to the devil. (Ephesians 4:26–27)

Jesus got angry without sinning. He had righteous anger. Righteous anger is not sinning. Jesus' anger led to the bettering of all people. Righteous anger toward evil, not people. Passive anger gives place to the devil. As believers, to "resist the enemy" (actively fight against) is a command, which is why at the same time we are called to "submit to God" (James 4:7).

The Embodiment of Truth

Everything Jesus is and was is identical to truth. In John 18, Jesus has an encounter with Pilate. Pilate starts the conversation by asking Jesus, "Are You the King of the Jews?" (verse 33). After a few more questions from Pilate, Jesus tells him, "My kingdom is not of this world. If My kingdom were of this world, My servants would fight, so that I should not be delivered to the Jews; but now My kingdom is not from here" (verse 36). The most profound thing Jesus says to Pilate is, "I have come into the world, that I should bear witness to the truth. Everyone who is of the truth hears My voice" (verse 37). Jesus was not merely establishing the existence of truth. He was affirming His embodiment of truth. If I reject what the Word says about love, kindness, and pain, I agree with a lie.

Every thought we encounter will have a God truth to apply. Our job is to search out the truth. God is kind because He doesn't leave us without the answers to our problems. His love offers solutions because "we have the mind of Christ" (1 Corinthians 2:16).

Through my healing journey and searching out the truth to defeat my past lies, I learned that how each generation speaks to the next affects what the young generation believes. Each generation continues to write the history for the future generations. In my family, I wanted to write a new story. One of freedom and not slavery. A story that didn't involve being addicted to alcohol, drugs, or porn. I refused to accept that addiction was going to be a part of my generation. What used to be can be set free through Jesus.

Knowing the impact of our words and how we speak to future generations, I thought about the Israelites and how an entire generation had to die before they could enter the promised land God had for them. Why? Because of a lie they believed.

Revelation of Truth and Freedom

The Israelites were enslaved in Egypt for several generations. Then God led His people to freedom and out of Egypt using a man named Moses. Unfortunately, in between slavery and the promised land was the wilderness they needed to cross. And suddenly, some of the Israelites decided maybe Egypt was a good place to live.

There are times when the Lord uses someone like Moses to reveal Himself to us, or the Holy Spirit brings a new revelation of the Word to us. When we receive a fresh revelation, the things in our lives that once felt heavy feel lighter. Fresh revelation brings insight we didn't see before into our story, which causes our lives to begin moving in a new direction. Who we once were becomes a new version we didn't know we could be. (Consider it an upgrade, growth, or maturity.) We enter a season in which we are discovering this new version of ourselves in Christ. Our hands are out, our palms are up, and we are ready to receive the promises of God. However, receiving a fresh revelation of God's Word can feel hard and unfamiliar, rather like a dry, scary wilderness. We want to retreat to our old way because our old way was a place of familiarity.

Slavery was familiar to the Israelites. When they entered the land they didn't know, and food and supplies seemed sparse, their desire for the comfort they once knew came for them and often won their hearts. The Israelites' comfort came through a normal routine, day in and day out.

Slavery wasn't what they wanted. Slavery was what the Israelites knew.

The wilderness—this new version of life they got to live—had too many variables. One example was God providing manna every day. God delivered enough manna for the day, encouraging the Israelites' hearts to focus on God and not themselves. He wanted them to know the manna was from Him.

> So Moses and Aaron said to all the Israelites, "In the evening you will know that it was the LORD who brought you out of Egypt, and in the morning you will see the glory of the LORD, because he has heard your grumbling against him. Who are we, that you should grumble against us?" Moses also said, "You will know that it was the LORD when he gives you meat to eat in the evening and all the bread you want in the morning, because he has heard your grumbling against him. Who are we? You are not grumbling against us, but against the LORD."(Exodus 16:6–8)

Through God's Word, we learn what His heart is for and what His heart is against. Knowing what God is for and against helps us see and understand what is of the Lord and what is not (the truth versus the lie). For example, when someone gossips about me, I want to gossip back and prove whatever words were said about me are not true. Yet God leads us in the other direction by saying, "Repay no one evil for evil" and "Do not avenge yourselves, but rather give place to wrath; for it is written, 'Vengeance is Mine, I will repay,' says the Lord" (Romans 12:17, 19).

The Israelites being in an unknown place, one not meant to be their place of habitat, reminds us that the depth of our pain can lead us to stay somewhere God never intended us to live. The Israelites didn't realize they were free from slavery and God was preparing them for a land overflowing with milk and honey. Their mindset and the lens through which they viewed their circumstances was from their past experiences: being slaves for many years. As we begin to examine ourselves, the same is true. Although set free (from shame, guilt, and curses of sin), our past can keep us from seeing the new life God has for us in Him.

The Israelites stayed in the wilderness because they believed the lie. And so do we.

Believing the Truth

Much like the Israelites had a hard time seeing God in their everyday lives amid the pressure they felt living in the wilderness, ten spies struggled to see God as bigger than the men they faced in order to take the promised land. God sent twelve spies to the land of Canaan, their promised land. After forty days of spying out the land, the spies came back with a report:

> Now they departed and came back to Moses and Aaron and all the congregation of the children of Israel in the

Wilderness of Paran, at Kadesh; they brought back word to them and to all the congregation, and showed them the fruit of the land. Then they told him, and said: "We went to the land where you sent us. It truly flows with milk and honey, and this is its fruit. Nevertheless the people who dwell in the land are strong; the cities are fortified and very large; moreover we saw the descendants of Anak there." (Numbers 13:26–28)

Looking at this passage, we can see the Israelites choose between a truth and a lie. The truth and the lie confronted them simultaneously, and they had to decide which they would believe to be truest for them. They would make a decision based on the lens through which they were viewing the report. The men in the land may have been strong, yet the lie was they were too strong to be defeated, as we will read.

God kept His promise in saying He had a land flowing with milk and honey. The enemy preyed on the Israelites' fear of man and their familiar place of slavery by saying the people who dwelled in the land were strong and the cities protected. To be clear, choosing truth doesn't mean truth will come without a battle. Standing on truth does not mean the easy way.

After receiving the report from the spies, Caleb quieted the people, as if to say he didn't understand all the chaos from the report. Caleb saw the land of milk and honey. Caleb saw the promise. He didn't say entering the promised land would be easy, and he didn't say there wouldn't be a fight. But the promise was true for him despite what he saw. He knew the battle was already won because of the Promise Keeper.

The Israelites viewed themselves "like grasshoppers" (verse 33). The Israelites' response also tells us how we view ourselves—where our worth and strength lie—can determine how well we show up in our lives. They didn't believe in God's promise. The Israelites felt small—minimal—in comparison to what was ahead of them. Then Joshua and Caleb came to remind them of the true report of the Lord:

> The land we passed through to spy out is an exceedingly good land. If the LORD delights in us, then He will bring us into this land and give it to us, "a land which flows with milk and honey." Only do not rebel against the LORD, nor fear the people of the land, for they are our bread; their protection has departed from them, and the LORD is with us. Do not fear them. (14:7-9)

Joshua and Caleb clung tightly to the words of God. Why? Because fear causes us to grip a lie so tightly that we cannot hold the fresh promises of God. When God is about to do a new thing, the devil tries to bring up old things. He wants us to look back when we should be looking up. Fear causes us to see realities that do not exist—realities in which God doesn't exist and defeat is the outcome.

Let's see the Israelites' response to Joshua and Caleb: "And all the congregation said to stone them with stones" (verse 10).

When we are clinging to the lies of our past, our rational brain gets turned off, and our fight-or-flight response takes over to protect ourselves. This can cause us to do and say things we may not mean.

Let's begin to close the story of the Israelites.

> Then the LORD said to Moses: "How long will these people reject Me? And how long will they not believe Me, with all the signs which I have performed among them?" (verse 11)

God is asking how long they will continue to need proof that He cares. Which leads us to ask ourselves the same question: How long will we continue to embrace realities in which God does not exist or a past that God says was covered through His Son, Jesus? How long will we wrap our hands around a lie instead of pursuing truth? The Israelites had a past. Their past was slavery, and their past infiltrated the truth, making the truth blurry.

God had a land of milk and honey. To take the land would take work. To win was to show up in obedience despite what they could see or what they felt. When we peel back the lies layer by layer, like an onion, we see more of the truth. God's Word is the only truth we need, and Jesus was the embodiment of truth. Anything apart from Him will not bear fruit.

———•❖❖❖❖•———

Truth leads us to repentance, redemption, and restoration. God's Word always brings good. How long will what someone said rule our hearts? How much longer will we allow ourselves to feel anger and jealousy?

When will God's Word begin to be more real than the emotions we feel or what our eyes and ears are trying to communicate with us?

Jesus knew no sin. God gave His Son so we could have life—a promised eternity in heaven and eternal life knowing God. Jesus became the curse so we could be reconciled to God, live in healing, and live well. Galatians 3:13–14 says, "Christ has redeemed us from the curse of the law, having become a curse for us (for it is written, 'Cursed is everyone who hangs on a tree'), that the blessing of Abraham might come upon the Gentiles in Christ Jesus, that we might receive the promise of the Spirit through faith."

The gift of grace through Jesus does not come with works. The wilderness is not supposed to be a desert we merely pass through. The wilderness is where God will birth fresh revelation in our hearts as we renew our minds from the slaves we once were under the ruler of this world.

When moving from bondage into freedom, pay attention

to the words people are speaking into your life, over your body, and about your circumstances. Be kind to receive the words that align with truth and rebuke what leads you away from God's redemption and restoration. Remember: The goodness of God leads us to repentance, and God's goal is always restoration, which produces healing.

CHAPTER / FOUR

The Healing Connection

I put my hand in front of my eyes to block the light from the police officer's flashlight through my window on the driver's side. I thought to myself, *Could I go to jail for this?*

With a slow movement, I put my hand on the button to roll down the window. As the window was rolling down, the police officer looked in my car. He could see Jack, whom I was dating at the time, in the passenger seat and Theresa, someone close to me, in the back seat of the car. The police officer proceeded to ask me to get out of the vehicle. As I got out, he took me behind my car and started asking me math problems and to do specific things with balance and my body. What he asked me to do next put me in a position I'd never found myself in before. "Get into the back seat of the police car, please," the police officer said. You can imagine the scene: He opened the door as I slid myself into the back seat. I was terrified, wondering how I had gotten to this place. Jack, Theresa, and I had gone to a water park to have fun for a few days over the weekend. Jack drank most of the day and never knew when enough was enough. I played along, wanting to be loved by a man, even though he didn't care how his actions or their outcomes affected me. Although I wasn't drinking and driving, the police officer smelled alcohol on him and in the car as soon as the window rolled down. I was guilty by association until he proved I wasn't.

The officer left me in the police cruiser and returned to my car, where Jack and Theresa were. I thought to myself, all alone in the back seat of the police car, *What have I done? How did I get here? This is not who I am.* Everything was happening so fast, yet it felt like time slowed down. *What is he asking Jack and Theresa? Why did he even put me in the back seat of his car? Were two more cop cars behind us necessary as we pulled into a gas station for missing my turn signal? What is going on?*

I was waiting for some kind of resolution to what was happening. The officer got in his car and started asking me questions. "Why are you visiting here? What are you doing out so late? Where did you come from and where are you staying?" I answered using the word *sir* and with fear trembling through my voice, "We are here because we are staying at a water park. We are visiting here. The bar in the hotel we were staying in closed and we decided to go out."

I continued to wait in silence after the officer finished

questioning me so he could run my license. He got out of his car, walked over to my door, and led me to the driver's seat of my car as he asked us to head back to where we came from. My world flipped upside down that night, because I saw what could happen if I continued to date Jack and if I continued to believe I had to fight for someone to love me by doing everything they did.

In the back seat of a police car, I had an awakening that would continue through my relationship with Jack.

For many years, I lived in an overwhelming emotional place where I thought everything happening in my life was a lesson. No longer were the days I searched for Jesus. I longed to find the answer to the lesson I was supposed to learn through my struggles. Feeling buried in my emotions, and wrestling with what I was experiencing, kept me in a constant loop of questioning who I was.

My normal was high stress, trying to do all the things so I could be something to everyone and avoid any more awful lessons. Trying to prove my worth and ability to others was normal for me. I worked multiple jobs so others would recognize how much I was doing. I wanted others to see how well I could handle everything without needing any help. I lived for the phrase, *Jess, how do you do it all?*

Busyness and stress are the way of life, many would say. The problem with this way of thinking is we normalize running ourselves ragged instead of realizing stress is common but not a normal state to live in for our entire lives. We were not created to bear high levels of pressure for long periods of time. When we normalize a frantic way of life, there's no reason to challenge that way of living. Soon enough, worry and anxiety become rites of passage and places that lead to exhaustion. The ability to say we can do all things becomes a badge we wear with pride. Your inheritance from accepting Jesus as your Lord and

Savior is not burnout. Accepting Jesus is receiving an abundant life.

This word *abundant* in the Greek is *perissos*, meaning "exceedingly, very highly, beyond measure, more, superfluous."[1] Jesus promises us a life far better than we could ever imagine. Let's look at 1 Corinthians 2:9: "What no eye has seen, what no ear has heard, and what no human mind has conceived—the things God has prepared for those who love him" (NIV). An abundant life is eternal life, but an abundant life is also being able to bring heaven to earth.

If we take a moment to consider the life we live, is going from one task to another without any rest or joy the reality we crave? When did constant racing thoughts, uncontrollable reactions, and being opinion-led become the norm? The more I listened to the world's advice, the more I began to live from a place of dread and worry—and the more of my awful "normal" I produced. My relationship with Jack proved my desire to be seen and recognized through my works. In other words, whatever came along, I accepted as is, without challenge. I thought all the craziness must be God's will for my life. There was no "But God's Word says this" to counter the lies and fear my life was stuck in.

Why does pursuing everything else in this world, like money, the perfect body, or our soulmate, never truly satisfy us? Because those things were never meant to satisfy our craving for being seen, connected, and loved. We believe the more we have, the more we will experience. Mark 8:36 reminds us of the cost when we gain all that the world has to offer. "What will it profit a man if he gains the whole world, and loses his own soul?" Why sacrifice our soul for momentary pleasures that are fleeting and empty? I learned through my busyness and depleted body that He wants our hearts, not our possessions.

---

1. *Strong's Exhaustive Concordance*, "4053, *perissos*," Bible Hub, accessed November 15, 2021, biblehub.com/greek/4053.htm.

The Healer of our souls created our bodies so unique regarding how we build connection, how we heal, and how our brains function.

Relational Change

Our brains have two sides: left and right. The right side is where we feel connection, relational components, identity and worth, emotional expression, nonverbal communication through the body, and imagination, to name a few. Our left brain focuses on logic, critical thinking, reasoning, conscious thought, and speech. Each side works together at the same time. However, one side of our brain tends to guide us more than the other—the logical side or the emotional side.[2] When I was trying to renew my mind by reading more, memorizing as much as I could, and striving to do all the right things they say we should do as Christians, I was trying to build a relationship with a relational God solely through my works, action, and reasoning. Trying to build a relationship through works is why I believe so many of us have a hard time living out the truth we read in the pages of our Bibles.

For example, believing God loves you may be a hard truth to live out. You may believe God loves everyone but you. You know your sins and are close to them. Therefore, you think to yourself, *How could God still love me for everything I have done?* Thinking God sees you through your sins causes you to work your way to His love, trying to make your life perfect. You think once your life is perfect, God will love you and you can partake in His will for your life. If our relationships here on earth hurt, cause us pain, or feel unfulfilled and empty, they become a clog in the pipe, slowly cutting off the flow from experiencing

---

2. "Left and Right Hemisphere of the Brain," The Human Memory, last updated November 25, 2020, human-memory.net/left-and-right-hemisphere-of-the-brain.

God in the relationship aspect. We tend to relate to God through our relationships here on earth. If our dad was an angry dad, we believe our heavenly Father is angry too. We look at the world and can see all the hate, and we believe God is a god of hate. The world we live in does not equal the kingdom of heaven and the nature of God. The kingdom way is the backward way. Living by the Word of God is to live in the complete opposite way of the world.

The good news is that God doesn't care about how much we know or do in His name; He wants to know if we know Him. Matthew 7:21–23 paints a clear picture of this for us:

> Not everyone who says to Me, "Lord, Lord," shall enter the kingdom of heaven, but he who does the will of My Father in heaven. Many will say to Me in that day, "Lord, Lord, have we not prophesied in Your name, cast out demons in Your name, and done many wonders in Your name?" And then I will declare to them, "I never knew you; depart from Me, you who practice lawlessness!"

The context of this scripture is that He is closing out His Sermon on the Mount by sharing a final warning about true faith. Jesus is reminding us that people will use all the right words, but they will not belong to the Lord. Jesus was not talking about knowledge in this scripture. He was talking about relationship.

God created us for relationship with Him. The further away we get from the unending love of our Father, the emptier we feel. That emptiness creates a gulf between our heads (what we know about God) and our souls and hearts (how we experience God).

Of course, renewing our minds is important. Scripture is clear about renewing our minds, but have you ever met someone who has been saved or known Jesus for more than ten or twenty years, who knows scripture but the scripture hasn't changed their actions or hearts? They may carry the same pain, the same hate, the same unforgiveness in their sous as if the events happened moments ago. Renewing our minds comes through relationship. When we have a relationship with God, our souls begin to change through scripture. We are becoming sanctified. We are denying ourselves and taking up our crosses to follow Him daily (see Luke 9:23). Relationships take conversation. Love takes sacrifice, obedience, and commitment even when we don't feel like doing any of those things.

Remember: We walk in the Spirit to deny the flesh. However, to live a deeply changed life, healing our souls and renewing our minds must go hand in hand. They are dependent on one another. The more we process through forgiveness, hate, and anger, the more the gap between our heads and our hearts closes so we can experience the Father's love. The more the gap closes, the fuller we fill with truth. Therefore, we cannot live by our actions alone or our words alone. Deed and truth must accompany each other. To read our Bibles but deny the process of forgiveness is contradictory, and we become double-minded and unstable.

Picture yourself having a splinter stuck in your finger. Splinters are little and almost invisible, yet they can cause so much pain when not dealt with. When we pull out the splinter, our bodies know how to heal. But if we never pull out the splinter, our bodies can't start the healing process, and we risk negative consequences, like an infection. We would never take out a splinter and try to put the splinter back into our skin. To heal—to have connection—we must recognize the splinter preventing our bodies from healing. By ignoring the splinter (pain, trauma, feelings), we run the risk of spreading an infection that festers into other areas of our bodies. One will always impact the other. Therefore, we have to ask ourselves what is standing in the way of our relationship with God and our deep connection with Him.

Head to Heart

Julie, a one-on-one coaching client of mine, spent twenty years of her life trying to find the perfect body, shaming her body, and being mad at herself for not being able to live out what she read on the pages of her Bible. "I know God's Word, but why can't I allow Him to love this out of me? Why am I continually struggling with shaming myself in this area? How can I let go of anger, frustration, and unforgiveness?" Julie asked. She came to me about food and her body. However, six weeks passed before we ever talked about either of those things. Why? Because Julie's frustration, anger, and sadness had nothing to do with her ability to eat right, move her body, or read her Bible.

Through our time together, she realized all the feelings she was experiencing were fruits of her childhood pain caused by words spoken by someone close to her. She was angry at her dad and the way he had treated her. Out of sadness toward the way her father treated her, she thought everyone wanted to treat her the same way her dad did. Therefore, Julie kept people at arm's length so no one could get close enough to her heart to hurt her again. She believed that every woman thinner than her must have an easier life and hadn't gone through any hardships like Julie had about her weight. She despised the thinner but rallied and championed the ones like her. Julie had head knowledge about God but no relationship at all. To her, opening herself up felt like stepping out into an enormous gap—where crashing into pain was unavoidable. But knowledge felt safe to Julie. She could look like she was pursuing God all while avoiding the possibility of a seemingly dangerous and potentially painful relationship.

During my coaching sessions with Julie, she came to the realization that no amount of Scripture memorization would close the gap from feeling to healing if she was not willing to allow God into her heart to tear down the fortress she built to protect herself from pain.

Julie was heavily left-brain-focused, meaning focused more on doctrine, logic, and reasoning. (The left side of our brain is also the conscious/verbal side.) The right side of Julie's brain impacts the left, but her focus was on consumption and works more than love and relationship (especially connection with people here on earth), which is her right side. But God created us with a beautiful connection between the two sides of the brain. Both are needed and required.

It would not be helpful for me to simply tell you to read more or do more without helping you also build healthy connections and relationships through love. God is both/and. God is relational as much as He is doctrinal (truth). This is why we can't use Scripture as a bandage; it must be ointment for the wound.

Fortunately, the Bible has a clear example of what the healing ointment of a relationship with Him can look like. Jesus had a relationship with His disciples. He was teaching, leading, and building a connection through conversation and breaking bread together. A beautiful, humble display of relationship occurs when Jesus washes His disciples' feet.

> When he had finished washing their feet, he put on his clothes and returned to his place. "Do you understand what I have done for you?" he asked them. "You call me 'Teacher' and 'Lord,' and rightly so, for that is what I am. Now that I, your Lord and Teacher, have washed your feet, you also should wash one another's feet. I have set you an example that you should do as I have done for you. Very truly I tell you, no servant is greater than his master, nor is a messenger greater than the one who sent him. Now that you know these things, you will be blessed if you do them." (John 13:12–17)

Jesus was showing the disciples humble, sacrificial love. He gives us the same task. We come alongside other people who have "dirty feet." Instead of criticizing them or shutting them down for their pain, we get to humbly "wash their feet." To wash feet is to have a relationship with another person. To have a relationship leads us to answer this question: Is love logic, truth, and reason, or is it relational, connection, and nonverbal? The answer is both/and.

My goal with Julie wasn't to fill her with more Scripture to memorize—because she already knew Scripture. The goal was to help Julie get the Word of God from her head to her heart. When we pursue God, His Word should transform our hearts as we renew our minds.

Realization

Self-awareness was the key for Julie to begin to transform her heart with God's Word. I walked her through taking inventory of the stories she believed and carried. For example, when she saw a skinny person, she assumed their life must be easy, while she struggled at the weight she was. Unfortunately, our internal narrative often impacts the way we see. Believing a story like this can only lead us to become bitter, envious, and jealous of others around us.

Since we cannot change what we are not aware of, Julie began to press into the area that terrified her the most: relationships and inviting people into her life. She became aware of the distance she had with others and started learning how to, brick by brick, deconstruct the fortress around her heart.

Julie knew Scripture. She could quote Scripture. But that wasn't enough. Julie needed connection, intimacy, and a willingness to be vulnerable enough to try again. Remember the healing connection is where we connect with God on an emotional and physical level. The healing connection occurs when both sides of our brain are being used. Here are a few questions to help you realize which areas need continued healing and growth:

1. Are you more emotionally based? Or more logic, doctrine-based? Why do you think that is the case?

2. How can you work to integrate emotions and logic together?

3. Do you find yourself being close to God but struggling with connection and relationships with people? Why is the disconnect there?

4. Do you avoid connection with people because connecting with others feels hard? If yes, why does connection feel hard?

5. Do you struggle to open your Bible because you don't know where to start? What prevents you from asking and reaching out for help?

6. What area in your life needs your attention right now the most?

7. As you read the Word, the Word should begin to transform your heart and heal your soul. If you have not started the healing connection, which area is the Holy Spirit showing you that needs tending to the most?

The more we focus on one and neglect the other, the more we miss the fullness of who Jesus is. He only did what He saw His Father doing, and He loved the people around Him while speaking the truth. He sat with people with whom others wouldn't waste their time. He constantly fought for those who felt isolated and cast out from what society deemed as good. Think about Him meeting the woman at the well. All this is relational, love, and truth. Both/and.

When pursuing healing, we need to experience the fullness of who God is.

The Lord has many names, but His name Jehovah Rapha means "the Lord that Heals."[3] Jehovah is the Great Physician who heals the physical and emotional needs of His people. We get to renew our minds, read the Bible, and know God as we connect intimately with Him and those around us. We are wired and created for love and connection, both of which, when done to honor God alone, can bring healing to our souls.

---

3. "The Names of God in the Old Testament," accessed May 6, 2021, blueletterbible.org/study/misc/name_god.cfm.

CHAPTER / FIVE

Addressing Your Whole Self

We can't hate our way into forgiveness. Forgiveness has compassion and empathy. Forgiveness lets go of the extra weight we carry.

I had a merciless point of view on forgiveness. No one was going to tell me I had to forgive someone. When I read about forgiveness in the Bible, it felt like a magnet repelling the same pole. No matter how much we try to put the north-pole side of a magnet with another north-pole side of a magnet, they will not go together. Forgiveness and I were repelling each other. Who would I be without the pain of my past? Who would I become without someone to blame?

I felt like forgiveness meant someone was "off the hook" for everything that was done to me. I had to continue to press into my pain through Scripture and the kindness of the Father to help me begin to forgive.

Do you recognize the cost of unforgiveness in your life?

For me the cost was how I saw the world and those around me, thinking people were always out to get me.

The cost was friendships and relationships, because I was bitter and angry.

The cost was trust.

The cost was chronic stress, because all my emotions from my thoughts were chemicals signaling throughout my body.

The cost was me dangling on the edge of a cliff, trying to hold a hundred pounds of weight, because I thought, *If the weight goes away, what would that mean about me?*

When I started the journey of forgiveness and healing from my past, I had known the Lord only a few years. I found myself doing all the "Christian checklist" items I thought I had to do.

Read my bible. *Check!*

Go to church. *Check!*

Tithe. Somewhat. *Half-check!*

My mind was learning about who God is, but my heart remained bitter, angry, jealous, and envious. I wanted everything God said I could have—peace, joy, forgiveness, and patience (to name a few)—but I wasn't willing to confront my heart or actions. I wanted everything without putting in the work. I don't mean action-based work such as creating the perfect quiet time or staying up to date on a Bible reading plan without missing a day (neither of which are inherently bad, but if we are not careful, we get so consumed with doing things right that we miss God in those things altogether) but the kind of work to heal the soul. The kind of work that calls us to slow down and pay attention as we walk through the stories of our past.

I lived in the tension of knowing what God's Word said I should look like and knowing I looked nothing like the words on those pages.

I spent most of my life waiting for God to give me peace, joy, and love. Scripture says we can't earn forgiveness. I somehow assumed that meant I couldn't do anything to make myself more like Christ. So, I left everything up to God. I did little to experience and know the Father on a deeper level. I waited to receive from God instead of searching His heart and mine to transform the way I lived my life.

Many people believe God can do amazing things and often quote, "I can do all things through Christ who strengthens me" (Philippians 4:13), but they experience little of His power.

They pray for peace, joy, and love, and to experience what the fruit of the Spirit has to offer but never experience the fruit of God's love toward them. If you're like me, you've wondered why. In my waiting for these feelings to come, I realized the part I was missing was responsibility and ownership for responding and reacting to the events and situations around me. I didn't take ownership of how I treated others or work on healing how others treated me. Every new experience that led to pain became a notch in my belt where I kept score.

Have you ever thought of God as a gentleman? I didn't either until someone mentioned this concept to me and it began helping me to see a new side of God. When I realized God is a gentleman, things started to change for me. I realized He was a gentleman when I stopped blaming Him for every bad thing happening in my life and realized that free will requires choice. His love is also by choice. God won't make me love Him. I get to choose to partner with Him and His love—or I can choose to partner with my flesh and the world. He won't do what we aren't willing to allow first. God won't make our mouths speak words of truth, kindness, or love over ourselves if we don't first believe them in our hearts. He won't force us to think on things above. Experiencing the fruit of God's love requires choice.

From the beginning, since Adam and Eve, there has always been choice. They could eat of the tree of life or the tree of the knowledge of good and evil. Why put the trees in there at all, you might ask? Because He wanted us to be able to choose. Still, today, with every thought comes our choice to choose Him or the lies from the enemy. God is love, and love requires choice. Would love be love if we were forced to choose it?

Choice

There is beauty in realizing we get to choose to heal. We get to take responsibility for our healing. God isn't holding out on us. He is available now—at this moment—and all that Jesus died for us to have is available to be received. Experiencing this new life in Christ isn't a matter of when, but if.

If we are willing to take responsibility for our choices, actions, and feelings, there is nothing He can't do through us.

If we are willing, He is ready.

Learning to partner with God has changed my walk with Him. When we begin to partner with God, we learn how to allow Him to work through us and not for us to work for God.

He already gave us everything we need. However, our responsibility is to work through the messiness of our hearts and deepen our relationship with Him. He's a good Father and a giver of good gifts.

Partnering with God

So how do we move from knowing we have what we need to real, lasting change and a relationship with God? We must first see ourselves as God does. In 2017, when my husband and I found our current church, one scripture transformed the way I see my entire self. First Thessalonians 5:23 awakened me to the fact that I changed when I said yes to Jesus: "May God himself, the God of peace, sanctify you through and through. May your whole spirit, soul and body be kept blameless at the coming of our Lord Jesus Christ" (NIV). The Message translation says, "May God himself, the God who makes everything holy and whole, make you holy and whole, put you together—spirit, soul, and body—and keep you fit for the coming of our Master, Jesus Christ. The One who called you is completely dependable. If he said it, he'll do it!"

Sanctify means "to set apart for a sacred purpose." The kindness and goodness of God call us up and out, not to live as the world lives. We are different, so we do not respond or react as the world does. Partnering with God takes our entire being—which begs the question: What does all of who we are look like?

First Thessalonians 5:23 says we are a spirit, we have a soul (our mind, will, and emotions), and we live in a body. Partnering with God requires all three. Let's take a look.

Spirit

Our spirit is our innermost part. We cannot see or feel our spirit. We can only experience the effects of our spirit. Our spirit is the main way to connect with God, and we can only use the spirit if we believe in God and receive Him through salvation. Romans 8:9 tells us if we do not accept Jesus, we do not possess the Holy Spirit: "But you are not in the flesh but in the Spirit, if indeed the Spirit of God dwells in you. Now if anyone does not have the Spirit of Christ, he is not His."

We receive His spirit when we receive our salvation. Romans 10:9 says, "If you confess with your mouth the Lord Jesus and believe in your heart that God has raised Him from the dead, you will be saved." Without being born again, accepting Jesus as our savior, we would not have a new nature: spirit. Before accepting Jesus, we had a sinful nature, and God cannot be a part of sin. We connect to God through our born-again spirit, which has no sin.

When we became a new creation in Christ, we got a whole new spirit. We were once slaves to sin, but now we are one with Christ. We were dead spiritually, but now we are alive in Christ. We used to belong to the enemy, but now we are God's property, and our spirit is sealed until one day when our body is redeemed.

> Therefore, if anyone is in Christ, he is a new creation; old things have passed away; behold, all things have become new. Now all things are of God, who has reconciled us to Himself through Jesus Christ, and has given us the ministry of reconciliation. (2 Corinthians 5:17–18)

Being born again means we no longer have a sinful nature; we have a sin habit. God's nature cannot coexist with a sin nature. We will still sin in this world, but not because the enemy has control. Works of the flesh means we flow from our human nature and what the flesh desires, which are evident in Galatians 5:19–21:

> Now the works of the flesh are manifest, which are these; adultery, fornication, uncleanness, lasciviousness,

idolatry, witchcraft, hatred, variance, emulations, wrath, strife, seditions, heresies, envyings, murders, drunkenness, revellings, and such like: of the which I tell you before, as I have also told you in time past, that they which do such things shall not inherit the kingdom of God. (KJV)

When Scripture comes out of our mouths, we are talking Spirit to spirit. As we speak Scripture, think on good things, and do what is right and true, we become aligned with God, allowing us to see His transforming power come through us (through our souls and into our bodies).

Picture a boat floating in the water. When an anchor is thrown overboard, hits the bottom, and locks in place, the boat will no longer be subject to the winds and the waves. The boat becomes subject to the anchor, because the anchor is keeping the boat in place. Although the boat might shift a slight degree from side to side and back and forth, the boat will continue to hold the position where the anchor was thrown.

God's Word is our anchor. When our spirit aligns with His, the Scriptures breathe life to the dead places in our souls. When our spirit aligns with His, it prevents our feelings from taking command of every situation. We will still have feelings, much like the boat still shifts slightly, but we will never leave our position, because God's Word points us to truth and healing to all circumstances. Our spirit plays an important role in the position our soul holds.

Realizing the enemy has no control over us frees us to take a stand against the lies that come our way from opinions, other people, our situation, or pain.

This is what flowing from our spirit looks like:

Soul (mind) → **Aligns with God's Spirit** (God's Truth) → **Through our spirit produces life in our body** (flesh)

Focusing on God's Truth through our spirits to produce life in our bodies takes a conscious effort within our minds and our thoughts.

Soul

Our soul is our mental and emotional part. Our soul can make up our personality. Our soul (thoughts, emotions) can only transform to the degree that we renew our minds, conform our values/priorities to the Word of God, and change our attitude. Romans 12:2 says, "And do not be conformed to this world, but be transformed by the renewing of your mind."

Paul also says in 2 Corinthians 4:16, "Therefore we do not lose heart. Even though our outward man is perishing, yet the inward man is being renewed day by day." In context, Paul has been talking about enduring death so life could come to others. He is telling the church of Corinth why he is willing to risk his life. Paul shares how his view of eternal life reduced his problems to "light affliction" (verse 17). He denied himself so others could receive, which takes us to verse 16. Paul's physical body, like ours, was breaking down and suffering adversity. However, his strength didn't lie in his body or whether people liked him or not. Paul's strength came from his belief about who he was in Christ. He received supernatural strength daily from God. Paul's soul—his mind—was so focused on God that what he saw didn't take up space in his heart. When God's Word transforms our souls, the problems of this world don't look scary.

I quoted Romans 12:2 over and over to remind myself to change my reaction time and the words I used, because the feelings I felt toward Dawn, a woman I went to church with, burned slow like charcoal in a grill. Until one day, my feelings ignited my heart and out of my mouth came words like a dragon breathing fire. I despised her words she used against me, treating me like I was a child and she was of God's spiritual elite (confirming the lie I wasn't good enough for God to use me). The part I hated the most was how my words were used against hers. I wasn't proud of my reaction or my response. I didn't want to be conformed to the world. I wanted to be transformed by the Word of God.

I realized transformation comes through spiritual renewing through God's Word. I recognized the more I created space with my emotions and making the world around me go silent, the more the enemy would sneak his way into my mind by telling me that what I was doing didn't matter. In the middle of silence and noise, I found tension. I found the battle for my thoughts that I left unattended for many years. The tension between the truth and the lies.

When I found the battle is when I recognized renewing our minds is one of the most crucial and important actions we can take in our walks with God today. Renewing our minds to God's Word is important because when our thoughts become aligned with God's Word, power is released. His goodness will be hard to experience if our thoughts consist of envy, jealousy, and anger.

Let's look at an illustration and imagine that someone robbed your house. He made a mess trying to steal things from you. Then you came home, and the robber left. Although the robber left, he left a mess in your house that needs to be cleaned up. In a similar way, you are now new in Christ. The enemy doesn't control you anymore—he's gone—but you are left with cleaning up and repairing what he tried to break. The enemy (Satan) has no control over you, because you have a very big, very powerful God hanging out with you in your house. But that doesn't mean Satan won't still come, try to steal things, and make an occasional nasty mess.

If we keep God close (by reading Scripture, praying, etc.) and fill our minds with things of God, Satan has a much more difficult time breaking into our house.

Before I learned about the soul's role, Scripture was somewhat hard to understand. We have new life in Christ, yet this new life didn't seem to change much from my old life. Paul writes in 2 Corinthians 5:17, "Therefore, if anyone is in Christ, he is a new creation; old things have passed away; behold, all things have become new."

Reading this verse can feel overwhelming and frustrating if we don't realize our spirits—the way we connect with God—changed at our new birth. After accepting Jesus as our Savior, we then spend our lives here on earth being sanctified and renewing our minds to God's truth. All this stems from our souls, which is our thought life. To sanctify something is to set it apart for special use; to sanctify a person is to make him holy. Sanctification is the process of becoming more like Christ.

The Message translation of Romans 8:29-30 is one of my favorite passages about who He created us to be:

> God knew what he was doing from the very beginning. He decided from the outset to shape the lives of those who love him along the same lines as the life of his Son. The Son stands first in the line of humanity he restored. We see the original and intended shape of our lives there in him. After God made that decision of what his children should be like, he followed it up by calling people by name. After he called them by name, he set them on a solid basis with himself. And then, after getting them established, he stayed with them to the end, gloriously completing what he had begun.

Reading this passage tells us that our original intended design is seen in Jesus. What a beautiful picture. However, I am sure many of us can relate to the fact we don't feel new or as if our lives have changed much since receiving Jesus. Our souls are the gateway to experience life and peace or death and destruction. The soul is the valve connecting to the spirit through and to the body. If we close the valve from the spirit, we become led by our feelings rather than by our faith. Think of our souls as the fulcrum of a teeter-totter. The fulcrum of the teeter-totter is the point where the beam pivots up and down. The fulcrum gives the beam the ability to pivot. On one end of the teeter-totter is our spirit and on the other end is our body. The fulcrum will pivot to whatever side we put more weight on, to accommodate the weight. Where we put our weight—our focus—our soul will accommodate and respond accordingly. If we pay more attention to our fleshly desires, they become more prominent in our life or our spirit. When we ignore God's Word, we are no longer dependent upon Him but instead allow ourselves to lead the way of what is right and wrong.

Our thought life can manipulate the emotions we feel and experience in our everyday life in the most basic way. The thoughts we think determine how we feel. Every time we think, we change (and train) the brain, and our body responds accordingly. (See more on feelings and emotions in chapter 6.)

The truth about our soul's role is this, what we think about dictates what we experience. What occupies our mind and thought life will eventually flow out of our lives. Living by faith requires patience, persistence, perseverance, understanding, and awareness.

This is what partnering with our body or spirit looks like from our soul perspective:

Body (flesh) ← **Soul** (mind) → **Spirit** (God's Truth)

Our soul (what we are thinking) determines what we partner with (our spirit or body). I began to experience more healing in my life when I believed God's Truth about healing and meditated on knowing He wanted to see me well. Speaking God's Truth over my body didn't end when I was experiencing physical symptoms. Bringing awareness to my thoughts and views of specific situations also changed the outcome of the situation. I learned we can't control what happens, but we can control our reactions.

Body

The body is our physical body—the part we can see, touch, and feel. Our spirit is new, but after receiving Jesus, we are still left with the body we had before receiving salvation. Our body is for us and not against us. God designed our body to follow our thoughts, which is why our thoughts are so important.

Our body responds to situations according to how we have trained it to. For example, remember how I reacted to seeing Rachel's name pop up on my screen? The years of manipulation and being afraid to stand up for myself often led me to accept anything anyone said about me or to me. I didn't want to deal with confrontation. Seeing her name reminded me of those moments, and my body began to shut down. I wanted to hide so I didn't have to deal with the confrontation I once knew.

God created our bodies to continue to protect us from future harm and pain. Therefore, our bodies have specific systems that control functions that turn on and off when needed. For example, when danger arises, our sympathetic nervous system response—fight, flight, or freeze—kicks in and decides whether we need to run, dissociate, or stay and fight. Our fight-or-flight responds to what is in our soul (mind), communicating to the brain in a few seconds and telling our body what to do. When I am in the ocean and seaweed touches my leg, I am out of the water faster than a running back runs into the end zone for the touchdown. Why? I have convinced myself, through story and beliefs, that seaweed will somehow drown me. My fight-or-flight response kicks in with a sign reading danger because of the story I believe about seaweed. Down to the smallest of details and thoughts, our bodies believe stories we think in our minds, which changes our brains.

Change in Prayer

Many times I prayed and then waited to see the answer to the prayer happen. However, I only believed God's promises were real—and my prayers mattered—if I saw the prayers answered, so I could have a tangible experience. God's Word was only real to me if I could see my prayers being answered. Faith wasn't in the unseen realm. My faith was only in what I could see in my body or soul.

The reality is the source of our truth cannot always be seen, heard, touched, and smelled. Truth isn't about discerning through our natural senses. What began to change my faith was to believe I had received when I prayed, not when I saw the answer. A powerful verse reminds us of this truth: "Therefore I say to you, whatever things you ask when you pray, believe that you receive them, and you will have them" (Mark 11:24).

The questions that linger on my heart and soul when I read Scripture are:

- *Will I believe God and know He hears and answers my prayers?*

- *Will I believe what I pray is done before I see the prayers answered with my physical eyes?*

If I depend on my body and physical senses more than I depend on God's Word and the truth of my new nature being identical to Jesus, then what I feel begins to rule my life (versus what God has placed in my spirit). To see my prayer life change, I had to align the words I spoke to match the Word of God. First John 4:17 confirms the beautiful truth that "love has been perfected among us in this: that we may have boldness in the day of judgment; because as He is, so are we in this world."

Our reality—what's in front of us—tries to dictate truth. One of our biggest influencers of unbelief is our five senses trying to rationalize the spirit realm. If we believe for healing and deliverance but don't "see" healing or deliverance, or experience it right away, doubt begins to form.

Praying for healing and then living what healing looks like in actions and words must accompany each other. Are you quick to respond to symptoms you feel in your body? How fast are you to react to your feelings? Walking out healing takes practice and awareness. For example, I used to pray for physical healing but would say how sick I felt and how tired I was, and I obsessed over weighing myself and taking my temperature. My words and actions rarely matched the prayers I prayed. How I was feeling emotionally turned into how I was feeling physically. Those were the moments I began to realize I could not separate parts of me. Every part of how God created me works together in unison. I want to be clear that God and prayer is not a formula. I am not saying the moments we align our words and actions with God's that instant healing will happen.

We can have truth to our reality and experiences while also holding the truth of God's Word above our reality. God's Word allows us to have control over our minds, will, and emotions. When we acknowledge God's Word remains true despite how we feel or what we see, we experience truth. That, in turn, affects our spirit and soul, which breathes life into our bodies. What changes is our interpretation of our present reality. Our interpretation starts to form by our beliefs, pain, trauma, and joy in our lives.

His Word is simple and true and not as easily lived out. I'm aware of the many parts of healing. I have become passionate about helping women address their souls. What we carry in our souls affects how we live in this world and how we view the world around us. Our beliefs determine what we see and how we see. Our words, actions, and thought life become some of the greatest places for us to start.

The more we begin to step out and stand on God's Word, the bolder we become in our faith and the more effective God's Word becomes in our lives. Everything in our life flows out of our hearts, including healing.

Psalm 147:4-5 tells us, "He determines the number of the stars; he gives to all of them their names. Great is our Lord, and abundant in power; his understanding is beyond measure" (ESV). Therefore, we can't keep trying to rationalize our circumstances to God's Word. Our focus should be taking God's Word to our circumstances until we see the promise in our reality. Of course, that takes perseverance and persistence. Hebrews 6:12 reminds us of this truth: "do not become sluggish, but imitate those who through faith and patience inherit the promises." When we turn to God's Word, His Word shows us exactly who we are in the spirit. His Word is a direct reflection of who we are.

———•••◆•••———

Our souls (thoughts and emotions) and how our bodies operate are like a perfectly designed, interwoven spider web with dew from the night before. The dew enhances every detail, angle, and pivot the spider spent hours creating. Our pain is the same. Our pain enhances the thoughts we have and impacts how we see our lives, just like the dew enhances our view of the fine threads of a spider's web. How we think about our bodies will begin to change our bodies. The actions we take follow the thoughts we think. For example, stress impacts many different organs in our bodies to respond and keep us running. Our body responds in the form of hunched shoulders, a headache, or fatigue.

The problem isn't that God is holding out on us when it comes to our healing. Sometimes we may believe we are not worth the fight to receive what He has already done for us (and wants for us). We are made in God's image, which means how we view God will impact how we view ourselves, another example of how one view will impact another view.

We may be able to act one way and think differently for a short time, but not at the cost or expense of something else. As we read through the Word, remember our spirit is already new, our soul needs renewal, and our body will eventually follow along for the ride.

CHAPTER / SIX
Understanding Feelings and Emotions

My life didn't change when I accepted Jesus. I accepted Jesus in 2010 when I was twenty-two. I started my ministry that year and bought a house. Before that, I was homeless with no place to call mine. My parents divorced when I was eighteen, causing division between my mom and my brother. Leaving my belongings behind, I moved in with my best friend to escape the pain.

Her parents took care of me as one of their own while I tended to anger, confusion, and constant thoughts surrounding why this was happening to me.

From there, I moved in with my cousin who had four kids, a husband, and a dog living under one roof. I lived in the basement, sharing a bed with my younger cousin. I learned to adapt and adjust because I spent most of my life running away from the pain and sprinting into the challenge that life would not bring me down. The year 2010 was one of transition without much change in my emotional position.

Some people have encounters with Jesus that change them from that point on, but not me. My relationship with God has been slow like a snail working to cross the finish line. Three years would pass after accepting Jesus as my Savior before I would read a whole chapter in my Bible in one sitting and two more years before I would even venture into the Old Testament.

I continued to believe everyone was against me, I was alone in the world, and I would have to hustle my way to the top. My actions toward people (which consisted of anger, bitterness, and a ruthless perspective on forgiveness) were the same as well. My life didn't change. Not because Jesus didn't provide a new way for me to live, but because I didn't understand what happened when accepting Jesus. I didn't know what having a new life meant. While I knew I had some worth, I didn't know where my worth came from. The Bible was more a book to read and know than a book to live and be transformed by.

I was at a place in my life where I had to begin sticking up for myself. My dating life was in ruins and run by men. I changed the music I listened to, how I did my makeup, and my views on life to match theirs. I reached my "enough is enough" point the moment Ralph, my boyfriend at the time, said, "I think you would look even better if you gained a little weight and had a bigger chest." However, in my quest to encourage women to know their worth, I didn't realize the depth of questions that would come with a simple phrase—telling women to know their worth spurred on more questions than answers. *How? How do I know my worth? What do I do when my boyfriend or friend treats me this way? I know I have worth but do not feel as though I do. Why? Why does God even care about me?*

Over the years, I realized saying "know your worth" carried weight and no longer became a cute bumper sticker or Instagram quote for me. Knowing our worth comes with deep roots tied to our identity in Christ. The emotional conflict we feel comes from the continuous overlay of the pain and beliefs we carry deep within our souls. Chapter 5 explained that our soul is our mind, will, and emotions. Therefore, bridging the gap requires our soul to be in tune with God's Word so the layers of pain and beliefs can be sifted and sorted. We move what's in our head to our heart and bury it deeply there. A transformation process happens every time we read the Word and move in the direction of the words we read. For instance, if I believed God had a better man planned for me, I had to set up nonnegotiable boundaries in my dating life. I had to allow God's Word to define my character to begin to put those character traits into action in real-life situations.

Without spiritual transformation, we only have behavior modification. Behavior modification is why many women I work with say, "I know what God's Word says, but I don't feel as though those words are true for me." The disconnect is beliefs, and the Word becomes blurry because of pain. We want to feel that truth is true. But we do not have to feel our worth and identity to know we have worth and a position in heaven. Knowing and feeling are different. Understanding the role our soul (mind, will, emotions) plays in our lives will help us discern between the two. Since our soul carries our emotions, knowing what emotions and feelings are helps us to get to the root.

Emotions

Emotions are chemicals released in response to our interpretation of a specific trigger. When we think a thought from an internal or external trigger, the thought creates an emotion. The emotion is chemical, and energy communicating through the rest of the body creates a feedback loop between the brain and the body. Emotions are important because they "continuously regulate every living cell to adapt to emerging threats and opportunities. They provide raw data about the world around us that is essential to our functioning."[4]

Our emotions become influenced by our memories, beliefs, and personal experiences. Emotions are neurological answers to an internal or external stimulus. For instance, say I spend a lot of time creating a post for social media. I am excited to post it, but when I do, no one likes or comments. I believe no one likes me. I experience the emotion of sadness, which leads me to feeling lonely, isolated, and misunderstood. Therefore, I turn inward and never want to share anything again. The trigger was no one liking or commenting. This led me in a downward spiral because I carried belief about the likes and comments that led me to experience the emotion of sadness.

Our emotions are triggered in two ways. One way is through an internal trigger. An example of an internal trigger would be meditating on past situations or imagining specific events. Even if a situation has not happened, if we meditate on the situation long enough, our body will begin to respond as though whatever we imagine

---

4. Michael Miller, "Emotions, Feelings, and Moods: What's the Difference?" Six Seconds, accessed April 30, 2021, 6seconds.org/2017/05/15/emotion-feeling-mood/.

has actually happened. Have you ever found yourself daydreaming about something that could happen, like a pay raise or someone in your family getting hurt? If we daydream about a pay raise, our bodies respond with joy and energy, and even go to the extent of dreaming all the new possibilities a pay raise could bring. Likewise, suppose we continue to think about something bad happening to a family member. Our body could respond with fear, and we might find ourselves suddenly feeling lethargic or having a racing heart. Neither one of those events happened, but our bodies respond to both as though they did.

We can make thoughts feel real when we aren't focused on what our external environment is telling us. Not focusing on our external environment helps to be able to have a single-minded thought. James 1:8 talks about being double-minded. In context, James is saying, "if any of you lacks wisdom, let him ask of God . . . But let him ask in faith, with no doubting, for he who doubts is like a wave of the sea driven and tossed by the wind" (verses 5–6). Verse 8 goes on to say that the man who doubts is "a double-minded man, unstable in all his ways." To be double-minded is to ask God but to ask in a doubting way. If we didn't have faith, we would not ask God at all. Without unbelief, we would not have doubting. Double-minded is the middle ground between our faith and unbelief. Being double-minded is why we have tension between what we know to be true and what we experience. As we move from faith to unbelief and unbelief to faith, our internal dialogue carries more power than we realize.

The second way our emotions are triggered is by an external stimulus. External stimulus means a real-life situation is happening in the present moment, and our bodies have to respond. Imagine someone is following close behind you. In a matter of a few seconds, you feel your adrenaline kick in and decide at a rapid pace whether you will run (flight) or stay (fight). You begin to analyze whether this person is a threat, and your palms may begin to sweat. You become triggered by a real-life event you did not dream up or imagine. Based on the information your body is receiving from your senses, your body will decide on what to do next.

Trigger (stimulus) → Belief → Emotions → Feeling → Reaction

Therefore, emotions are set into motion by an internal or external stimulus—a trigger.

Our emotions promote bodily reactions, such as increased heart rate, facial expressions, or sweating. To sum up, our emotions tell our bodies what to feel.

Feelings

Feelings, then, are the conscious experiences of the emotional reaction. They are the physical and mental sensations that arise as we internalize emotions. Feelings are cognitively saturated emotion chemicals. Feelings are necessary because "feelings are how we begin to make meaning of emotion; they cause us to pay attention and react to the perceived threats or opportunities. We're acting on emotional data."[5]

When we say that "our bodies hold stories," this refers to the narratives our minds believe about every pain, trauma, or moment in our lives. Every event we experience carries a story of joy or dread. The past stories our bodies hold become the reference guide for current events. Every moment, our bodies respond in the ways we have trained them through our beliefs, pain, and joyful moments. Good news: If we have trained our brains and bodies to respond one way, it means we have the strength and power to train

---

5. Miller, "Emotions, Feelings, and Moods."

our brains in a new way. Feelings become sparked by emotions shaped by our personal beliefs or memories.

Thoughts are the language of the brain, and feelings are the language of the body. You can become subconsciously triggered by something someone said or an event. Therefore, you react and respond according to who you have experienced in the past or the story you have told around it.

We can't escape what's in our souls and hearts. Proverbs 27:19 paints a beautiful picture of this for us: "As in water face reflects face, so a man's heart reveals the man." There is no separating the two. They go together because our body works as one. We can't escape or run away from what we feel because the root of our emotions is what tells us what to feel.

The problem with our feelings is they are fickle, not facts, and they change consistently based on each scenario in our lives. To get what we feel under control, we must understand our souls—one part of our souls being the thoughts we think.

God created us to be thinking and emotional beings. He gave us the power and authority through Jesus to use our words to speak life (see Proverbs 18:21). When I was physically recovering from being sick, I spoke to myself things like "God redeemed your life from destruction. He crowns you with lovingkindness and tender mercies. He heals all your diseases. He satisfies your mouth only with good things" (see Psalms 103:2–5). My body was trying to tell me that I was tired and would never recover, so I should just accept this "sick" life. But Scripture tells us "the things that come out of a person's mouth come from the heart" (Matthew 15:18 NIV). Whatever is in our soul—our thought life—determines how the world around us changes and looks.

Our minds and brain are not the same. The brain is passive and the physical part of our body we can see, whereas the mind is active and something we cannot see. The mind is our thoughts and memories.

The good news is God hasn't left us defenseless or powerless in our thought life. God is the Healer. His Word is healing. He tells us how to think, what to think about, and what to avoid. His Word tells us we have power and authority over our feelings. The thoughts we think have to submit to the Word of God. Through Scripture, God tells us to hold every thought captive and put those thoughts into submission to the Word. He wouldn't call us to put our thoughts into submission if He didn't provide the authority to do so:

> For though we walk in the flesh, we do not war according to the flesh. For the weapons of our warfare are not carnal but mighty in God for pulling down strongholds, casting down arguments and every high thing that exalts itself against the knowledge of God, bringing every thought into captivity to the obedience of Christ. (2 Corinthians 10:3–5)

Through Jesus, we have been reconciled with God and given authority to pull down strongholds, cast down arguments and imaginations, and dismiss every thought that doesn't align with God's truth.

The truth about our soul's role is this: What we think about dictates what we experience. What occupies our mind and thought life will eventually flow out of our lives. Living by faith requires patience, persistence, perseverance, understanding, and awareness.

The Impact

To understand the impact, we have to go back to our past. We are spirits with a tender soul at home within a body where all parts communicate together. Our past is no mystery to God, but our past can guide us through our present responses. The more we look at our past to learn about our present, the better we can equip ourselves.

Our present response has a lot to do with how our past experiences have trained our parasympathetic and sympathetic nervous systems—parts of our physical bodies. The sympathetic nervous system controls our fight-or-flight response. Our sympathetic nervous system acts like a green light that says, "All systems are ready to go and respond." The sympathetic nervous system triggers our fight or flight response, which tells our body how to respond to the current situation in front of us that we are dealing with. Should we run? Do we stay and fight? Is now the time to shut down and draw away? Understanding my fight-or-flight response allowed me to begin to have compassion for myself.

Learning why I responded to certain situations a particular way allowed me to understand more about my response to others and how my body was responding to pain kept inside. For example, when I would see my husband, Jon, resting on the couch while I continued to work, blood would start pumping through my veins and into my heart. My thoughts would run wild around the fact that he was resting while I was working. My body was responding to a lie I believed that if I didn't do whatever tasks needed done, then no one would. This was my way of surviving. I thought I had to take care of everything in my life myself because of the memories from my past.

Fight or flight is our body's response to survival. Our sympathetic nervous system is what drives the fight-or-flight response. Its response is to stimulate cortisol and adrenaline to mobilize us to fight or to flee from danger. The amygdala interprets the images and sounds, and then sends a signal to the hypothalamus. The hypothalamus then communicates to the rest of the body, through the nervous system, how it needs to respond. We can view the hypothalamus like a command center.[6] When we are in a constant state of stress, and talking about how stressed we are, our bodies never leave a state of fight or flight. Our body protects us at all costs and is preparing for battle. Suppose our brains continue to view situations as dangerous. In that case, our brains will continue to send signals to our bodies, traveling to the pituitary glands, which release hormones that trigger the adrenals to produce cortisol.

Sometimes the smallest things can trigger emotions that fill us with regret. White-knuckling is an example of how we might try to push (and rush) through the day, experiences, and our everyday life. If we were in a game of tug-of-war, we would have our hands wrapped around the rope so tightly because we do not want to lose. In our attempt to win, we grip so hard our knuckles become white and the rope beneath our palms burns our hands. We may white-knuckle our life consciously or unconsciously, but we ignore the warning signs from our brains and our bodies that God designed specifically to help us cope. A few examples of this are ignoring hunger pains, apologizing for our feelings, and minimizing our feelings as not being so bad—or maybe a Netflix binge or picking up our phone more than a hundred times a day to distract ourselves.

Understanding fight or flight at its most basic level is essential to understand why we show up the way we do in certain situations. Learning how our body responds gives us the ability to pull away and into healing. God didn't create us to live this life by "just getting by." He came for us so we may have an abundant life. Even with the stress of this world, we get to live from a place of peace and a sound mind. Living in past experiences and emotions as if they are happening now can directly impact our health.

---

6. "Understanding the Stress Response." Harvard Health, July 6 2020, health.harvard.edu/staying-healthy/understanding-the-stress-response.

These experiences and our beliefs about them can impact how we live in the present and our future reality.

There might be times when we do not realize when this is happening. Still, we may begin to notice an increase in heart rate and blood pressure, or we may begin to feel anxious.

When we live in fight-or-flight mode, we cannot connect to the areas of our body that give us the ability to problem solve and to reason. I spent most of my life relying on the same coping way that I always had: defense, which is our fight-or-flight response.

Our bodies tell the stories of our souls.

Future Reality

When challenging situations or experiences come up, or when we remember them, the response we have is a signal showing us our bodies want to move into the direction of healing. When the signals arise this is the way our bodies begin to tell the stories. Paul writes in Philippians 1:6 about how God will continue to do a good work in us: "Being confident of this very thing, that He who has begun a good work in you will complete it until the day of Christ Jesus."

Once again, this is a beautiful example of how God created our bodies for healing and wholeness. God gives us comfort in the form of sweet reminders from His Word.

Living constantly in a fight-or-flight response isn't supposed to be a way to live our lives. The fight-or-flight response was designed to protect us from danger, not to protect our souls.

I have said that our bodies are among our greatest storytellers. God created our bodies to provide valuable feedback to us as we begin to experience those stories. Through our experiences, we start to form beliefs about our identity and our worth. If the experiences do not filter through the lens of God's love and His Son dying on the cross, we end up living a life stuck carrying our pain and versions of ourselves (from other people) that were never ours to carry alone or forever.

Understanding our nervous system will help us work through specific parts of our life that are overwhelming or feel like "too much." Healing emotionally can lead right into some physical healing as well. Knowing why our body responds the way it does allows us to begin to have kindness toward ourselves as we start to go deeper in the areas that maybe we have kept hidden for a long time. We may try to ignore it, but our body doesn't forget.

My body never forgot the desire to have its basic needs met like affection and comfort. I would do anything to feel those desires, retreat when the pain began to feel too much, and remind myself often I had to keep going no matter the cost. I would have one boyfriend lined up before I broke up with the boyfriend I was currently dating. Not having someone there felt like I was being abandoned, which drove my need to never be alone. Mentally I tried to act tough and as though I had my life together. Acting tough was my way of keeping people at arm's length—so I wouldn't feel like I owed them anything. I had a tough exterior, but my soul was slowly dying of loneliness and not feeling loved or taken care of.

Our future reality is not dependent on our history. To heal is to learn how to reframe our past so our pain does not hinder our future. The future we have with God has nothing to do with past mistakes, the things done to us, or how well we perform. What we do next with God will depend solely on our relationship with God Himself. Paul, in Philippians 3:13-14, reminds us to look forward, to look up to heaven, and not on the road behind us: "Brethren, I do not count myself to have apprehended; but one thing I do, forgetting those things which are behind and reaching forward to those things which are ahead, I press toward the goal for the prize of the upward call of God in Christ Jesus."

There is beauty in honoring our past stories without them becoming our identity, our worth, the lens we view the world through, or our future. Our past may be trying to tell us something right now (according to how our body responds and reacts with fight or flight). However, we get to continue to press toward the prize: the upward call of God toward healing.

CHAPTER / SEVEN

Changing Your Mind

Every tear that streamed down my face onto the pillow felt like a weed ripping from my soul. As they rolled down my cheeks, I closed my eyes, wanting the pain to go away and to be on the other side of what the Lord wanted to do in me.

During this part of my healing journey, His Word felt like sandpaper rubbing all the wrongs places. The sandpaper (His Word) was rubbing against the callus I built around pride, arrogance, and self-righteousness.

Pride, arrogance, and self-righteousness came at an early

age. I grew up at sixteen. That's the first time I can remember believing that if I didn't take care of myself, no one would. At sixteen, I got my first job, bought my first bed, bought my lunches at school, and learned to trust no one at their word who said they cared for me.

I learned at a young age that when someone did something for me, their kindness toward me needed to be reciprocated when they needed me. Therefore, everything people did for me was nothing more than a tally added to their sheet to keep record of my rights and wrongs against them, which led me to not depend on anyone for my basic needs. If I had them met by someone, great. If not, I let it roll off my back like water rolling off a duck's back.

Every time I was confronted with kindness from someone, I always had in the back of my mind that I did not want to owe this person later. Every act of kindness dug that lie deeper. The lie is that when people do nice things, it's only for their benefit. This would be why I spent most of my life hating to receive gifts. To receive meant to take, which meant to owe.

As God's Word continued to feel like sandpaper against my calloused heart, I knew God wanted to create something new in me, much like the psalmist asked for in Psalm 51:10: "Create in me a clean heart, O God, and renew a right spirit within me" (ESV). I could see broken pieces of my heart in His hands. He chiseled every piece that I deemed unfit and unworthy, taking the old broken piece and creating something new.

I had a lot to learn about the broken pieces I kept handing to God. *How do I depend on God when I have depended on myself for a long time? Can I change and be transformed into the design He has in mind?*

God doesn't want to take your broken pieces and mend them back together. He wants to take the pieces and design something completely new.

Through the Lord's kindness, I began working on training my thoughts. Now I recognize when my pride or arrogance rears its ugly head, when past trauma causes me to slip into my old patterns of thinking and reacting. As soon as I recognize what I am experiencing, I begin to speak to my sixteen- to twenty-something-year-old memories. I remind her she is cared for and loved. In these moments, my thoughts are pliable. I consciously think about my reaction in the present versus when I was experiencing something I didn't understand in the past.

Think a Different Way

In moments of confusion when past hurts resurface, it's important to remember the lessons of 2 Corinthians 10:4–5: "For the weapons of our warfare are not carnal but mighty in God for pulling down strongholds, casting down arguments and every high thing that exalts itself against the knowledge of God, bringing every thought into captivity to the obedience of Christ."

The weapons of our warfare are not carnal—of the five senses. Nothing in this physical realm truly puts Satan back in his corner like the Word of God does. The weapons of our warfare are mighty in God. His Words are our weapon. Although simple, it is not an easy truth to remember or apply when all of who we are becomes dominated by the responses from our trauma. The KJV says in verse 5, "Casting down imaginations," while the Message says, "We use our powerful God-tools for smashing warped philosophies, tearing down barriers erected against the truth of God, fitting every loose thought and emotion and impulse into the structure of life shaped by Christ."

Basically, God is asking us to stop imagining the worst. Instead, He says, if we are going to imagine, why not imagine a life not filled with sickness or emotional turmoil at every corner? Why not imagine ourselves enjoying our lives with our friends and family, and not being exhausted afterward? Why not imagine living a life of freedom, not chained to the feelings of anger, resentment, and jealousy? Why not? Our lives will not change until our thoughts change. A ship can turn by a single small rudder. If someone changed the direction of the rudder by one degree, over time, one degree of change could lead them completely off course. Therefore, our tongue is the weapon for our warfare. What we consistently speak over time matters. I love how the Message words how powerful our tongue is in James 3:3–10:

> A bit in the mouth of a horse controls the whole horse. A small rudder on a huge ship in the hands of a skilled captain sets a course in the face of the strongest winds. A word out of your mouth may seem of no account, but it can accomplish nearly anything—or destroy it! It only takes a spark, remember, to set off a forest fire. A careless or wrongly placed word out of your mouth can do that. By our speech, we can ruin the world, turn harmony to chaos, throw mud on a reputation, send the whole world up in smoke and go up in smoke with it, smoke right from the pit of hell. This is scary: You can tame a tiger, but you can't tame a tongue—it's never been done. The tongue runs wild, a wanton killer. With our tongues we bless God our Father; with the same tongues we curse the very men and women he made in his image. Curses and blessings out of the same mouth!

Our tongues can only speak what is already forming in our hearts.

Change is hard in the beginning. Even though the old way of living still brought on stress, worry, and shame, renewing our minds is challenging because the lies feel like the path of least resistance, and the truth is fighting to change the course. When truth meets a lie, there is opposition.

When we decide to renew our minds, change stirs the waters. Correction stirs the spirit realm around us, and the spirit in us becomes alive. The enemy now knows we are aware of his deceptions, so the pushback becomes harder, because the last thing the enemy wants is for us to be free from the emotional bondage we have allowed ourselves to be under for far too long. With the additional freedom, God's Spirit in us will continue to become more alive and apparent. More of His truth replaces the lies, and you become more like God.

So then, as hard as it is, the opposition is a sign of good, forward movement toward truth.

Allow the opposition to come.

Hard Change

When I began to learn how much the pain I carried affected every other part of my life, I was desperate for answers. How could I make what I knew to be true something my soul accepted as fact? A popular scripture I have already referenced is 2 Corinthians 10:5: "Bringing every thought into captivity to the obedience of Christ." Many of us would probably follow this up with "But how?" Sometimes we want a spiritual answer that feels long and hard. Sometimes the answer is simple but requires more effort, intention, and patience.

Basically, if we continue to think the same way and live the same way, our brains will repeatedly fire the same neural patterns. In return, hardwiring our brains to believe and live one way means that if you continue to think the same thoughts, behavior, or feelings, they will become automatic and unconscious habits. We will reproduce the same reality without giving too much thought to change. For example, have you ever been driving in your car and, when you reach your destination, you don't remember getting off the exit? Our body takes over because our mind remembers.

When our external environment influences us that much, our external environment becomes our source of truth over God's Word.

When we live by our senses, our thoughts are limited to the events we are experiencing.

To live by faith is not to live by our senses. We do not deny our senses exist or ignore what they are trying to tell us. However, living by faith is not knowing the outcome and believing anyway. Choosing to live in faith is believing in what's beyond present events. To live by faith means to hold His promises regarding what He has spoken about our current situation or circumstances.

God challenges and calls us to change our minds, not just to think positively.

Neuroscience would call focusing on a different thought or reality *mental rehearsal*, but as a woman who loves Jesus, I call mental rehearsal meditating on God's Word. The Word of God should create a vision in our hearts that gives us the ability to stand when our lives want to knock us down.

These few scriptures remind us how important meditating on His Word is:

> You will keep in perfect peace those whose minds are steadfast, because they trust in you. (Isaiah 26:3 NIV)

> Keep this Book of the Law always on your lips; meditate on it day and night, so that you may be careful to do everything written in it. Then you will be prosperous and successful. (Joshua 1:8 NIV)

> I will meditate on Your precepts, and contemplate Your ways. (Psalm 119:15)

As we begin our healing journey and meditating on the truth, the lies will come for us. The enemy will fight us even more because we are challenging the lies we believed to be true. Our brains and bodies have been firing chemicals and neurons to support the lies (the pain and story of our past), and because we have a real enemy at work trying to uproot the Scripture within us.

As we begin to open the doors of our hearts and embrace them with kindness and compassion, we start this process of pruning old thought patterns that have fired together so we can begin to form new ones. Pruning old thought patterns leads me to John 15:1–8:

> I am the true vine, and My Father is the vinedresser. Every branch in Me that does not bear fruit He takes away; and every branch that bears fruit He prunes, that it may bear more fruit. You are already clean because of the word which I have spoken to you. Abide in Me, and I in you. As the branch cannot bear fruit of itself, unless it abides in the vine, neither can you, unless you abide in Me. I am the vine, you are the branches. He who abides in Me, and I in him, bears much fruit; for without Me you can do nothing. If anyone does not abide in Me, he is cast out as a branch and is withered; and they gather them and throw them into the fire, and they are burned. If you abide in Me, and My words abide in you, you will ask what you desire, and it shall be done for you. By this My Father is glorified, that you bear much fruit; so you will be My disciples.

Abiding in Him produces fruit. Apart from Him, there is no good fruit. Without Him we can do nothing. When Jesus says He takes away, He's pruning the parts of us that do not bear fruit—maybe old ways of thinking, old patterns of behavior, and things keeping us from seeing or experiencing Him.

He's not taking things away to punish us or to make us mad. Old ways of thinking, old patterns of behavior, and things keeping us from seeing or experiencing Him keep us cast out as a branch and withered. Think about this practically for a moment. When we meditate on how upset we are, how someone wronged us, anger from our childhood, or how stressed we are, what kind of fruit do we produce in our body? We might experience something like digestive issues, headaches, an inability to sleep, tight neck muscles, or fatigue. When our mind thinks about joy, good report, or love, on the other hand, what kind of fruit do we produce in our body? Meditating on joy might lead to more energy, better sleep, or improved digestion. Old patterns get pruned, new routes get formed, and our mind changes, which means our brains change and, in return, new chemicals release.

Rewiring

It's as simple as this: If we want a new feeling, we must think a new thought. Then we must repeat that new thought until it becomes the new habit.

Think of it a bit like a computer motherboard. A motherboard controls and connects all the computer details. "It is the spine of your PC, it is the link between all the different components inside your computer. One of the major functions of a motherboard is to act as the 'hub' to which other computer devices connect."[8] Now picture a motherboard with all its wires leading to a specific path. The path we choose leads to a part of the motherboard that controls a specific part of the computer. If those wires didn't lead to the right path, the computer would malfunction.

---

8. "How Computers Work? Motherboard," Prezi, accessed November 15, 2021, prezi.com/p/mhfukzvgynza/how-computers-work/?frame=abe96a57935591cf67a66178fa84c38a07f86adf.

There are circuits in our brains that link to certain feelings and emotions, causing us to respond in particular ways. Every feeling we have carries a habitual action. When those circuits in our brain link to pain, the emotions and reactions that come out look more like a malfunction than an adult reaction. The only way to function properly is to pull out the old wiring system and rewire our thoughts so our new thoughts communicate effectively with our bodies and align with His Word. Our bodies are always communicating with our thoughts.

Mind Alignment

How do we take our thoughts captive? Aligning our souls with God's Word produces life and peace. We will not experience peace when our thoughts and actions focus on the problem, the symptom, or the circumstance. Of course, God created our emotions and senses; this is not a call to deny our senses. Our senses, however, cannot be the engine that drives our choices—especially regarding our feelings. Our feelings should never be what lead us. Feelings can't be what guide our life, and they can't get the final say. We need to make sure they do not become a part of our identity. If we are unwilling to "see" what can't be seen yet in this world, walking by faith will be hard.

> Now faith is the substance of things hoped for, the evidence of things not seen. (Hebrews 11:1)

Experiencing more of Him (His power, wisdom, and healing) requires us to be in faith for things we cannot see yet but know them to be true because His Word says so. You and I received Jesus as our Savior "by grace . . . through faith—and this is not from yourselves, it is the gift of God—not by works" (Ephesians 2:8–9 NIV).

The type of seed we plant reproduces after its own kind.

The more seeds of truth we plant, the more truth will become rooted in our thoughts, and our bodies will reap the benefits of life and peace. Everything Jesus did on the cross has nothing to do with our performance.

Grace means we are free and no longer sin-conscious. Free from sin not to sin.

Now is the time to begin to step out of trying to be perfect and into our newfound freedom with Jesus' grace. We no longer have to punish ourselves with our thoughts, calling ourselves screwups, failures, unworthy, and whatever words the enemy uses against us to convince us that who we are and what Jesus did are never enough. Something powerful we need to remember is that Jesus became what we were so we could become what He is: righteous (see 2 Corinthians 5:21).

We are either partnering with our flesh or our spirit. Galatians 5:17 says, "For the flesh lusts against the Spirit, and the Spirit against the flesh; and these are contrary to one another, so that you do not do the things that you wish." Our thoughts and emotions can lead us to envy, jealousy, strife, and more, which produces its own fruit like headaches, body aches and pain, or fatigue. Or we partner with the spirit, which leads us to "love joy, peace, longsuffering, kindness, goodness, faithfulness, gentleness, self-control" (verses 22–23).

I'll never forget the time I listened to Susie, an acquaintance, tell me how much harder than mine her work is, and how she has to have the best nails and the perfect clothes. She continued to speak to me as though I had no clue what I was doing in business and my business was worth less than hers. With every ounce of me I wanted to prove who I was and list the people I knew and the places I have gone, so I could prove my worth to her. While Susie was going on and on about how amazing her life was, I began to check in with myself. I was in the process of training my mind and brain to look at situations objectively and with different points of view. How would my reaction help or hurt? Would pridefully telling her my points change her heart about who I was? Why was she talking and sharing these things with me? What was going on in her life and what was she feeling?

When we take a moment to step out of our emotions, we can get a clearer picture of the scene. Think of wiping bugs off a windshield: pride was one of my many sight-obscuring bugs.

I could have chosen to partner with my pride and works of the flesh. But I chose to pursue peace and fruit of the Spirit. My thought life (my soul) hinged on the part of me I was going to give the most weight and control to.

There is no denying when our thoughts align with His, the power in us—through Him—gets released into our bodies. When our thoughts (soul) focus on and align with God's Spirit, our spirits produce fruit. Then you experience a fruit of the Spirit. Experiencing God's Word is no longer about the works we do or the feelings we feel. Receiving this kind of love and healing means what we do—our works—has nothing to do with what Jesus did for us (His death). We don't have to work our way into love and healing.

Scripture tells us we have the mind of Christ. I love how the Message translation describes 1 Corinthians 2:10–16:

> The Spirit, not content to flit around on the surface, dives into the depths of God, and brings out what God planned all along. Who ever knows what you're thinking and planning except you yourself? The same with God—except that he not only knows what he's thinking, but he lets us in on it. God offers a full report on the gifts of life and salvation that he is giving us. We don't have to rely on the world's guesses and opinions. We didn't learn this by reading books or going to school; we learned it from God, who

taught us person-to-person through Jesus, and we're passing it on to you in the same firsthand, personal way. The unspiritual self, just as it is by nature, can't receive the gifts of God's Spirit. There's no capacity for them. They seem like so much silliness. Spirit can be known only by spirit—God's Spirit and our spirits in open communion. Spiritually alive, we have access to everything God's Spirit is doing, and can't be judged by unspiritual critics. Isaiah's question, "Is there anyone around who knows God's Spirit, anyone who knows what he is doing?" has been answered: Christ knows, and we have Christ's Spirit.

Practical Change

Once our mind becomes aligned to God's Word and truth, how do we begin to change our minds and our brains? Review the "Rewiring" section of this chapter (p. 104) to be reminded how our brain is like a motherboard in a computer. Here are six ways our minds and brains can change.

1. Learn something new or acquire knowledge.

Presenting our brains with a challenging environment or learning a new task requires our brain to do something out of our normal track. The body will begin to adapt with consistency to the new task, skill, or knowledge. When we feel frustrated learning something new, it's a sign our brains and bodies are adapting. When I started to learn how my mind worked, and began to read books on healing from childhood trauma and recovering from being an extremely pessimistic person, I felt unintelligent. I felt as though something was wrong with me. Every time I tried to learn about renewing my mind or focusing on Scripture, I could not retain what I was learning. I would pick up a book, read a few pages, and try so hard to make the connection. Whatever I was reading felt like another language. I thought I would never be able to understand. Don't give up in the moments when change seems hard. Our brains are creating new routes. Our thoughts are still important during this process of change. Remember: our minds change our brains. I love how our heavenly Father is kind to guide us into new territory within our minds and thoughts: "I will instruct you and teach you in the way you should go; I will guide you with My eye" (Psalm 32:8).

2. Try hands-on instruction.

Hands-on learning changes the brain because it "better engages both sides of the brain. Listening and analyzing processes occur in the left hemisphere, but visual and spatial processes are handled on the right. By combining multiple styles of learning, the brain forms stronger overall connections and is able to store more relevant information."[9] One step I took to make Scripture come alive was to rewrite Scripture in my journal. I was not only reading Scripture but writing down what I was reading. Then I added in drawings to what the Scripture was saying or explaining. I was allowing myself to learn in different dimensions. Beyond drawing, I could, for example, build a train switch to visually see what changing our thoughts to new patterns and routes look like. We can add layers to drawing and even listen to Scripture being read to us while we draw. Some Sundays when my pastor talks, I find myself drawing the words and phrases he is repeating, or I draw arrows connecting pieces in a flow to help me better remember. When we feel stagnant in our learning, maybe we need to change how we are learning instead of giving up altogether. All of us operate differently, but we all have

---

9. Jonathan Arnholz, "Is Hands-On Learning Better?" Build Your Future, February 12, 2019, byf.org/is-hands-on-learning-better/.

the same power (through Jesus) and control as believers to put our thoughts into submission.

3. Focus on thoughts.

The more we pay attention to a thought pattern, the more our body will learn that pattern. Therefore, we have to be careful not to strengthen thought patterns we would not want to see come to life in our reality. For example, imagine we were in a room together, and someone placed a bin of red, green, and yellow flags in front of us. The person who placed the bin in front of us asked us to count how many red flags we could see. Then they took the bin away. The next thing this person asked us to do is to tell them how many green flags we saw. We probably wouldn't have an answer, because we had not been focusing on the green flags but rather the red ones.

Where our attention goes matters. Now let us look at how this scenario could apply to Scripture. If we put our focus and attention on God's Word, our brains will begin to change because our attention is on His Word. Scripture will fill our thoughts. If we focused on nothing else besides Scripture to define us, our situations, and our feelings, nothing else would be magnified. Psalm 119:15 says, "I will meditate on your precepts and fix my eyes on your ways" (ESV).

4. Write for clarity.

After we bring awareness, paying attention to the details from those thoughts and what they formed, we want to process them out on paper. Writing can help us bring clarity to our thoughts. Getting creative in our expression of what we are feeling helps us get out exactly what we have been thinking without a filter. We get so overwhelmed because our thoughts become like pulling Christmas lights out of a box in December. Everyone knows untangling Christmas lights is one of the least-enjoyable parts about them. Our thoughts are much like Christmas lights in our heads: they are running every which way, and there seems to be no end to the mess we feel through our thinking. Getting out a piece of paper and journaling through the thoughts we bring into our consciousness might help us untangle the wires in our brains and think more clearly. No one likes a tangled mess of cords. Our brains don't either.

5. Take action.

There is a difference between deciding to forgive someone and actually forgiving someone. There is a difference between deciding to believe in God and actually believing in Him. The difference is acting. James paints a clear picture of action for us in chapter 2, verses 14–18, 26:

> What does it profit, my brethren, if someone says he has faith but does not have works? Can faith save him? If a brother or sister is naked and destitute of daily food, and one of you says to them, "Depart in peace, be warmed and filled," but you do not give them the things which are needed for the body, what does it profit? Thus also faith by itself, if it does not have works, is dead. But someone will say, "You have faith, and I have works." Show me your faith without your works, and I will show you my faith by my works. . . . For as the body without the spirit is dead, so faith without works is dead also.

As we read through this passage, we notice James doesn't mention when we feel like believing to then move in faith. Faith isn't seeing. Faith is believing. Faith is not living by what we feel. As you bring clarity through writing, pray for God to bring clarity to the areas that need the most attention. God is kind to show us names, events, and character changes we need to focus on to search out the truth to them in Scripture. If we are angry about something and our thoughts expressed the emotion of anger, what does the Bible say about anger? We get to search out (take action) and know the truth about what we feel without anyone's opinion.

6. Repeat the good things.

Relationships build on repetitive conversation. We don't have one conversation with someone and call that a relationship. Our brains work the same way. Our brains need repetition to signal change. Every thought we think builds on the others. The more Scripture we build in our hearts, the more Scripture will come out of our mouths. We speak out of the abundance of what is in our hearts (see Luke 6:45).

A psychological principle states that "what fires together, wires together." Whatever thought we take hold of and pay attention to will only grow as we feed more thoughts into whatever we are thinking. If we do not focus on a specific thought pattern, we tell our brains that thought pattern is no longer important. Over time, the thought pattern will be forgotten, and our thoughts will become wired to our current route of thoughts. Think of awareness, attention, clarity, and action all together playing in a movie. Every thought pattern has its own movie that requires awareness, attention, clarity, and action. With every thought pattern, we watch the movie play out before our eyes. When we close our eyes, we can picture ourselves turning off the movie, walking to the TV, taking out the DVD, and putting in a new movie. The new movie is our new thought pattern. Therefore, we have to continually pursue change to experience change.

There are times we blame our inability to change on motivation or the willpower we think we don't have.

Our brains learn in different ways. Try something new, see how the different learning styles feel, and keep pressing into the uncomfortable part of growing and learning in a new way.

Sharing how our brains change is only one piece when we want to learn to renew our minds. Another important piece is understanding how our thoughts and feelings come to be on the most basic level. (Review chapter 6 for more on feelings and emotions.)

We are one with Christ and in right standing before Him. God is not looking at how we feel to determine His love for us.

The new way of thinking becomes our new way of living.

CHAPTER / EIGHT

The Rework

I was on a red-eye flight home from a business conference when I woke from a deep sleep. My head felt foggy, my body began to radiate warmth, and I felt as if I were looking through scratched lenses. I decided to get up and use the restroom, and the next thing I knew, I was waking up on the bathroom floor of the airplane. I didn't know it at the time, but I had hit my breaking point. I didn't realize how bad the stress and emotional burnout had become until my pancreas failed me on the flight home. Now my body was beginning to experience the effects of my afflictions. It had gotten to a point where I had numbed my pain for so long that when I began to finally feel again, everything felt intensified and bigger, like looking through a magnifying glass.

My breaking point led me to months and years of discovering my denial of stress, overwork, and trauma. Yet, the words "God is giving you this to teach you a lesson" left me with weak knees, a head bowed in shame, and hands that spent hours looking for what He was trying to teach me.

It left me feeling I wasn't good enough when I kept hearing that God wanted me sick to teach me a lesson. My view of the Father was someone who was handing out sick passes to His children to teach them to become better listeners. It impacted how I viewed myself. I didn't want to go to the Healer for healing because I thought He wanted me to be sick. Believing this lie kept me sick longer. Eventually I began to know of a Father I had never heard of before, a Father who wanted me well, and that began to change every fiber in my being. Knowing the Father started to change who I thought I was in Him to who I was in Him: a woman of worth capable of being well.

This led me to question why I numbed my pain for this long. What was at the root of all this? These questions led me to Luke 6:43–44, which reads, "For a good tree does not bear bad fruit, nor does a bad tree bear good fruit. For every tree is known by its own fruit." The part of the scripture that stood out to me the most was that every tree is known by its fruit. Whether the tree produces good fruit or not, the tree is still known by its fruit. Our lives resemble the tree. I asked myself, *What kind of fruit am I producing and reproducing in my life?*

When we think of a tree, we know dirt and food (fertilizer and light) are required for the tree to live and survive, much like God's Word is required for us to live a righteous and holy life. As a tree gets older, the deeper and bigger the roots get, and the more branches the tree grows.

Standing next to a tree, we cannot observe how deep the roots grow. The tree has its roots in the ground, the trunk for support, and the branches that hold the leaves. We can tell what kind of fruit the tree will carry with everything we can see about the tree.

Although we may not be able to tell a fruit of a person by looking at them, we can tell by the words they speak, what is happening in their lives, what they are experiencing consistently, and their actions.

When we are young, our memories, experiences, and traumas are minimal. Our experiences change from childhood to adulthood. The roots of a young tree are similar: They are not fully developed or have the strength they will in ten years. Years go by for the tree to mature. Our childhoods help us form many of the viewpoints we carry into adulthood. How we grew up, were treated, and were spoken to shape how we see, act, and talk as adults in this world.

Those memories, experiences, and traumas become the thoughts we think; they can form our identity and the base of who we are. When we think of a tree trunk, we think of a sturdy, strong base for the tree to grow and blossom. Our thoughts and experiences are our base. They determine whether we blossom, how we blossom, and what fruit we bear. As we get older, much like a tree, our base gets bigger. We have more thoughts and more experiences.

Our thoughts determine the emotions we feel. Trees have many branches. Think of these branches representing the many different emotions we can feel based on our thoughts. The more thoughts we begin to have, the more we will begin to experience them in reality.

The emotions we feel begin to affect every area of our life. Now, think about the little branches that extend off the tree's main branches. Those little branches represent the different areas of our life affected by our emotions, whether good or bad.

Let me break this down a little bit more.

Memories, experiences, traumas, and God's Word equal the roots of our life in which everything starts to form.

When we begin to create thoughts around those memories, experiences, traumas, or God's Word, from our roots we form the trunk. Our thoughts formed become the base of who we are. Our identity begins to take formation by our thoughts, which are the branches.

Then our thoughts form our emotions, which is the fruit of the root. With every experience, memory, trauma, or piece of God's Word we meditate on, we create a new thought that leads to an emotion. Good or bad—we can experience many emotions.

Therefore, the memory, experience, trauma, or God's Word created a thought, leading to an emotion that will begin to affect every other area of our life.

Feelings aren't bad unless they become like longhorn beetles. Adult longhorn beetles lay eggs in an opening in a tree's bark. The larvae then bore large galleries deep into the wood. These "feeding" galleries disrupt the vascular functioning of the tree and eventually weaken the tree to the point that the tree literally falls apart and dies. If we focus on our feelings versus the Word of God, they become destructive, disrupting our connection to God, and we become weakened and disconnected from the Vine.

When expressing feelings with love and truth, people experience the kingdom.

With this, we can begin to understand how important renewing our mind to God's Word is and how our pain and feelings can start to build on one another over time. Our minds try to suppress memories to protect us, so it might take some work to dig into our memories.

Redirecting

As my feelings began to build on each other, someone came into my life when I least expected it. Her name was Sue. We worked together at my first and only full-time job, at Jo-Ann Fabrics, a place where God taught me patience, obedience, responsibility, and love. Sue was like a caring grandma you wish you could snuggle up next to at every family get-together and listen to her tell stories.

There would be days I would show up to work in a ball of tears due to the ending of a relationship, a fight between my parents, or when I felt like a broken girl that had no safe place to call home. Sue would not only listen, but she would guide me with her words, telling me that I didn't have to live in the pain. She began to redirect my pain by her acts of love. Sue would give me gifts of money and tell me to get something fun or food for myself. She taught me kindness without expectation. Her acts of love redirected my anger and slowly began to soften my heart. She would always say not to make the mistakes she did and to learn from hers. It's been ten years since I left Jo-Ann Fabrics to work from home full-time, and Sue still sends me birthday cards with cash, telling me to enjoy it and how proud she is of me.

Without Sue realizing, she opened a new circuit for me that was never open before, one with patience and understanding. She became like an orchestra in a grand symphony teaching me the most beautiful rhythms of grace.

When we want to rewire our minds to a new circuit, we need to learn and repeat the step of redirecting our train of thought. Sue provided many moments of redirection for me. However, we are with our minds 24/7. Redirecting our thoughts is our responsibility.

For a long time, my emotional life looked like weeds. My emotions rarely produced fruit that was good. My soil was full of opinions and pain, which led to growing rotten fruit. My emotions consumed me. I continued to water the same soil, expecting to produce a different kind of fruit. However, a seed can only produce after its own kind. I hardwired my brain to believe the lies as truths without ever challenging the beliefs that I had become aware of.

Awareness

First John 3:20 serves as a reminder that God is greater than our feelings and knows every detail about our hearts: "For if our heart condemns us, God is greater than our heart, and knows all things." We can't run from Him, and He never hides from us. Knowing He is greater brings us comfort because He is our source of truth, not what we feel. When we know God never leaves us, even in our turmoil, we realize that time will not fix what we are going through; we must pursue healing.

Time can soften the intensity and frequency, but time doesn't make what we feel go away. Feelings do not just go away. They transform into something better or bigger. The goal is to create space between us and the emotion to focus our souls on God's truth.

The following five steps make us aware of our emotions as they come:

1. Acknowledge the emotion.

Stop for a moment. When we begin to feel our heart start to race, our palms start to sweat, or like we want to cry or run, take a moment to acknowledge that our bodies are communicating something with us. Our bodies are responding to a current situation by past information. Our brains have a catalog of events. Imagine a Rolodex. Each card has information about every situation, event, and circumstance in our lives. In addition to a detailed description of what happened, each card includes a lot of notes reminding us how good or bad the particular situation, event, or circumstance was for future reference.

Every time we get triggered, internally or externally, our brains go through the Rolodex, turning the wheel and flipping through the filing system, so our brains can tell our bodies what to do next, according to something similar that happened in our past. Taking a moment to pause and recognizing that something feels different or off allows us to bring our thoughts into consciousness. Acknowledging something isn't right reminds me of James 1:19–20: "So then, my beloved brethren, let every man be swift to hear, slow to speak, slow to wrath; for the wrath of man does not produce the righteousness of God." There is kindness in slowness. We are kind to ourselves and those around us when we take a moment to pause and reflect.

2. Identify the emotion.

Is fear, anger, or envy present? Once we acknowledge something isn't right, we can give ourselves permission to explore what we are feeling. Is this hindering or serving us? For example, when we experience fear as an emotion, we will have feelings of being afraid, frightened, or scared. When anger is our leading emotion, we will feel anger or rage. If envy is our emotion, we will feel resentment or be unhappy.

Identifying the emotion is the tripwire—the trigger—which allows us to begin to feel so we can move toward God's truth about what we are experiencing.

> God has not given us a spirit of fear, but of power and of love and of a sound mind. (2 Timothy 1:7)

Even when we feel we have the power to put what we feel into submission.

3. Accept the emotion.

Acceptance allows us to feel without being run by what we are experiencing. I have learned we are run by our emotions when we run away from them. I stayed in a relationship with Hank for two years too long because I ran from my fear of being alone. Instead of dealing with why I was worried about being alone, I allowed the fear of being alone to drive my decision-making. I stayed with Hank not only because I didn't want to be alone, but because I could not bring myself to break up with him because he was a nice person. I reasoned and evaluated all the time: *But Hank is a good person.* I continued to deny everything I knew I should have been doing while running from my emotions, which amplified everything I should not have been doing. I refused to accept being alone.

Refusing to accept being alone left me in a loveless relationship for two years too long. I was on the run. When we choose to accept what we are experiencing in the moment we are experiencing all the feelings, we stop ourselves from running. When we refuse to run, we can evaluate why we are experiencing what we are feeling. We may have feelings, but what is the truth to what we feel? We can feel sad, but feeling sad does not make us sad people. Having anger doesn't make us angry people. We cannot let what we feel become an "I am" statement in our life. God is the only one who gets to say who we are and what we are made of.

4. Recognize what the emotion is telling you.

As we have learned, there are stories surrounding what we believe. They could be true, or they could be lies. Truth brings healing and restoration. Lies produce death and cause us to wage war in our souls. We must ask ourselves, "What is this emotion trying to communicate to me about who I am? What are my circumstances showing me?" Often what we are experiencing emotionally opens the door to the areas of our life that need healing, repentance, or renewal.

Our bodies are the best communicators to what is going on inside of us. Honor that. A slow response gives us precious space. Romans 8:13 tells us the importance of not living according to the flesh: "For if you live according to the flesh you will die; but if by the Spirit you put to death the deeds of the body, you will live." Without getting to the root of the trigger, the fruit we try to grow in our lives will eventually be ruled by the flesh and die.

5. Have a conversation with God.

Our last touching point in awareness is our conversation with God. How do we continue to move toward healing (versus continuing the cycle of this feeling)? It may feel hard, uncomfortable, and awkward. However, interrupting our normal thought patterns to create new ones founded on the truth of God's Word is how we renew our minds. Changes happen in tension. We create tension when we think a new thought in opposition to what we used to think. The healing hand of God can be felt in these moments.

To change the way we think, we must challenge the way we think. Think of a railroad switch. A railroad switch allows the train to be guided from one track to another. The interruptions of a normal thought pattern, the conversations with God, and the truth we bring cause us to switch tracks and take a new route. At the meeting point of the switch is where we will feel our greatest tension.

These awareness steps could happen in a matter of seconds, or they could take some time to get used to. The more we put these steps into practice, the more we recognize what is happening within us as things are happening around us. Kindness and grace toward ourselves are important during this process, much as they are during planting and harvesting. In between planting and harvesting are tilling the ground, watering the soil, and giving the soil everything needed to produce good fruit for harvest time.

Whenever we learn something new, the beginning comes with frustration and feeling confused. Tension means there is a breakthrough happening. The tension we experience doesn't mean what we are doing isn't God's will for us. Breaking through the tension means we are living from victory, knowing victory is already ours. If the enemy can keep us down, he will. Friction means we are awake and not settling anymore into a life that God has never asked us to live.

Our brains and bodies have believed one way, maybe for a long time. The roots to the lie go deep. Healing is going to take time. Healing will be a process with layers. Every layer pulled back invites maturing, growth, and closeness with a Father we never experienced before. A baby isn't expected to run before they can walk. A baby finds their footing and holds on to the end table to find balance in standing before letting go to walk and eventually run. Every stage is important for growth and maturity.

There is not a step or action too small that the Lord won't use for good. When we are willing to surrender everything we have over to Him, He can shape our souls to look more like His heart.

Chasing God will lead our feelings into submission.

> He who trusts in his own heart is a fool, but whoever walks wisely will be delivered. (Proverbs 28:26)

When we take hold of thoughts, our brains assign meaning to those thoughts, creating the emotion, thus creating the feeling. Emotions last seconds, but feelings can last a long time. To deny our emotions exist is to deny the way God created us. God is love. Love is an emotion and involves emotion. God intended emotion for good. Experiencing the fullness He has for us through our emotions and feelings is to know there is responsibility in maturing, growing, and producing them.

Learning there is a responsibility to do the work is a stepping-stone for us to no longer need to be validated by what we feel. We do not need an experience to know God loves us. Our feelings will come and go. On the days when we do not feel God, it doesn't mean He left.

There are promises written in His Word encouraging our hearts about how close He is. The promises God wrote to Abraham and Joshua are the same promises for us today. Here are a few scriptures to meditate on:

> Be strong and of good courage, do not fear nor be afraid of them; for the LORD your God, He is the One who goes with you. He will not leave you nor forsake you. (Deuteronomy 31:6)

> Behold, I am with you and will keep you wherever you go, and will bring you back to this land; for I will not leave you until I have done what I have spoken to you. (Genesis 28:15)

> No one will be able to stand against you all the days of your life. As I was with Moses, so I will be with you; I will never leave you nor forsake you. (Joshua 1:5 NIV)

He is with us, reminding us we do have control and a choice over our thoughts because of Jesus. To serve God with all of who we are, we must not become reliant on our emotions to tell us to. God created us with such purpose. We can see this in the fine details of our emotional response. Understanding our emotions and feelings helps us to feel equipped for the new adventures this world gives.

CHAPTER / NINE

Emotional Safety

I grabbed the hammer to confront the red brick wall in front of me. With sweat dripping down my eyes, I felt my stomach twist and turn as an overwhelming sense of both fear and relief settled into my body. I clenched my jaw tight while my shoulders held tension to hold my feelings.

The hammer shined like the sun reflecting off of a newly waxed car with a grip that kept my hand at ease and firm. I turned to the wall. My eyes stared straight ahead as I began to think to myself, *Is this hammer going to be enough to break through the wall between me and where I know God wants me to go?* With shortness of breath and my knees lacking strength, I took the first swing. Only but a few pebbles came off the wall.

I swung the hammer again, but with more force and a faster speed. More rocks fell when I realized force, strength, and striving would not be what would take this wall down.

I laid the hammer down as I sat, leaning my back against the wall and realizing the wall my back was leaning on consisted of layers of bricks I formed around my heart. The red brick wall I was confronting was me. The wall I was facing was what I built around my heart so no one could hurt me or see my weaknesses.

No amount of exertion could speed the process of getting to the other side of the wall. Only faithful, steady swings would chip away at the precise spot to take away the brick layers one by one.

I wanted to fight to get to the other side of the wall because feeling anger, jealousy, and bitterness were the feelings I was running from even though those feelings built the wall. I thought if I could work my way to the other side of the wall, whatever was on that side would take care of itself; I was hoping everything would disappear.

I could grab something else with substantial weight like a sledgehammer. Wouldn't a sledgehammer (striving to change everything all at once) do more damage to the wall? Yes, a sledgehammer could do more damage quicker, but the Lord isn't interested in how fast I go but how steady I stay in my swings. He wants me focused on Him as I take His Word (the hammer) and tend to my bricks (pain) in the wall around my heart. "'Is not My word like a fire?' says the LORD. 'And like a hammer that breaks the rock in pieces?'" (Jeremiah 23:29).

We know what walls do, right? Walls create separation and division. Walls can divide two areas of our life that should be intertwined together. Soon the house we build around our heart has so many walls we can't find our way to the door where we can knock so the door will be opened (see Matthew 7:7). Within our hearts, we build this fortress of a house with many walls as dividers. All the dividers cause us to be divided between people and distant from God.

Striving to find our way back leaves us breathless and exhausted from running. He is asking, "Will you keep the pace with My word despite how fast and far the world wants to take you quicker?"

The Word is like a hammer to break down the wall. Still, the Word is also sharper than any two-edged sword, which Hebrews 4:12 reminds us: "For the word of God is living and powerful, and sharper than any two-edged sword, piercing even to the division of soul and spirit, and of joints and marrow, and is a discerner of the thoughts and intents of the heart." Like the hammer, God's Word begins to break down the wall. His Word also enters our heart and begins to pierce through the vile thoughts, disrupted nervous system, and an overtired body to bring rest. God is a discerner of thoughts and intents of the heart. How we see the world, relationships, and God often stems from how we were raised and are treated here on earth.

So I sit at my walls of fear. I stare at my walls of pride. I lean into the walls of feeling unseen. All the tending to my walls has left the outside of my house overgrown with weeds, run-down, and barely noticeable.

We can't keep building walls while growing in intimacy with the Father or building healthy relationships with people. The closeness, comfort, and safety we desire from relationships will not be met when no one can get through our door. Even though we try to convince ourselves we won't allow pain to happen again, we must realize the depth of love we have and experience is the depth of pain we can feel. To love is to know trust can break, people will use their words against us, and forgiveness will be a process. To love is knowing God can restore trust in us, relationships can be redeemed, and restoration is readily available.

No matter what our walls try to tell us—such as they are safe, they are comfort, they keep people at arm's length enough to be kind and loving but not enough to allow ourselves to experience or receive love—our walls don't have to keep building, and the fortress around our hearts doesn't have to be where we live forever.

The Journey to Safety

On my quest to break down the walls around my heart, I recognized the process to allowing others in would require safety and trust. When I met my husband, I lived in Ohio, and he lived in Pennsylvania. The drive was a little more than two hours each way for us to see each other. Since we both committed to not live together before marriage, there was a lot of driving back and forth. Therefore, much of my "living to survive" mode remained throughout our dating and engagement. I still depended on myself more than anyone else during those times in my life, including the One who will always provide.

There were security and safety in the predictable day in and day out of my tasks. What was in my bank account allowed me to feel safe; my being able to control how clean my house was and what went where felt comfortable. There was no one to challenge my day-to-day routine or the thought life I had created until I got married and lived with my husband. Not too long after marriage, I hit a wall and realized my prideful sin. In feeling like I had to do everything and be someone to everyone, I took on all the cleaning and everything else. I was going to do everything, so I could make sure everything was done right. I was pridefully self-reliant and that gave me a measure of safety: If I didn't depend on anyone, I could ensure I was cared for properly. In other words, no one could hurt me.

I knew pain was present in my heart, but I didn't realize how much I depended on myself to take care of me until my husband wanted to love me and asked me to let him share in parts of my life. Learning how much I relied on myself also made me realize how much I needed God to tend to my prideful heart and hurried life. Not too long after, I realized I didn't believe God was a safe place for me. Letting in someone I couldn't physically see felt too risky, no matter how much He said He loved me.

Between the poverty of my childhood and the pain of dating an alcoholic, a sociopath, and men who didn't quite have their lives together, I no longer trusted anyone but me to be the provider and the protector of self. Even though I wasn't technically alone, there wasn't a place where I felt seen, heard, or cared for. God created our bodies to heal, and He wants us to move in the direction of healing. But we also need a safe place to start the healing process. Not long after getting married is when I was safe, body and soul, for the first time. Ironically, after getting married, I started to show real symptoms of the pain and trauma I had endured.

My body knew relaxation was okay, there was no immediate danger, and I could begin to process the reality and experiences around me. This conclusion led me to realize my ability to heal emotional wounds as an adult is not dependent on my parents, friends, or men. As an adult, I could allow God to heal those wounds, whether anyone else recognized, validated, or tended to them. Our healing isn't dependent on others' repaired connection with us.

Safe Place to Land

God is the only one who doesn't have to mend a broken relationship with us, so He is the safest place for us to deal with our pasts. Jesus already reconciled our relationship with God. Even before the reconciliation, God loved us, which is why He sent His Son to die for us. He loved us so much that He didn't let us continue wallowing in sin. He wanted us free from the curse. God becomes the safe place for our emotions, situations, feelings, and trauma to land because He is the ultimate pain-taker who sent His Son to pay the ultimate price. He is safe because His love is not conditional, He doesn't keep score, and He shows us a way through our pain.

While His love for us has not been on trial, our love for Him has. These are questions to ask yourself to determine what you may need at this moment and moving forward:

1. Do I feel like the feelings I express matter or are important to the people in my life?

2. Do I feel safe sharing what I am feeling with the people to whom I am closest?

3. Do I feel that what I share may only cause guilt or shame, so I choose not to say anything at all?

4. Am I often talking about how stressed and overwhelmed I am?

5. Do I try to fill my time with something to do? For example, at a red light, do I pick up my phone? When going to the bathroom, do I feel I need my phone? When there are moments of silence and stillness, do I try to fill those moments with something instead of experiencing the silence and stillness?

For every question you answered yes, think of specific moments when you felt like you mattered, when you felt safe, unhurried, and not busy. For the questions you answered no, think about the comments or situations that made you feel like you didn't matter or didn't feel safe. Examine the areas of your life that constantly leave you feeling stress and overwhelmed. We cannot change if nothing under the surface changes. To change, we must know where the roots are. We need to know why we feel God isn't safe.

These questions are to get us thinking deeper and reveal struggles we might otherwise not recognize. When we think deeper, we can begin to ask the Holy Spirit for guidance. Day by day and moment by moment, we have experiences. If we aren't willing to slow down long enough to embrace, challenge, or question the experiences (to discern the truth), we will not be able to learn how to trust God with our life. When we are not willing to look at our lives, nor embrace the experiences and stories we carry, how can we give them to God and lay them at His feet daily? Embracing the truth that God is a safe place to land requires us to remember the Creator of the world created us on purpose. He is safe because He never changes and is not disappointed in us. He will lead us to whom we may need to reach out to talk or where we may need to start saying no. Asking ourselves these questions allows us to go beyond our regular routine of thinking and helps us to look deeper to examine the roots of our actions or responses.

Safety in Being Known

I talked to PJ, my spiritual father, almost every month for six years. After getting married, our conversations grew less frequent. Although my husband, Jon, is now my safe place, PJ was the one who stepped up to take a father role in my life when my heart was searching for answers from my younger years. At a time when I was struggling to deal with my past, I received a text from PJ that read, "Hey there beautiful! In my life there always has and always will be a spot for you. I'm still very protective of you. It's a dad thing." He went on to say, "Please read this as an openhearted invitation to accept love. You are dear to me."

It wasn't that I needed PJ's approval or that my husband's or God's love wasn't enough. However, God is kind to bring people into our lives who will speak life to the dead places in our hearts that may have felt robbed or not 100-percent comfortable (safe)—if we are willing to listen. God is number one in tending to my emotions and feelings, and in validating who I am.

PJ's words reminded me I was still known to him and not someone he forgot. Even though his role looks different now, he's still a safe place for me.

Every season of life will look different and have different people taking the role of offering a safe place. But we should be conscious of how much we rely on different people based on how safe they are for us. I love to look at this through layers. If we draw a circle, the first circle will be God. The next circle, drawn around the first, will be those closest to us, like our friends and immediate family. The third circle could be connections we have, such as our neighbors and acquaintances. We can continue the circle with people we do not know but may come in contact with. Each layer or circle holds and carries a level of influence in our life. The closer in the circle to God, the safer we feel with those people. God is the ultimate safe place because He's with us everywhere we go. We can't escape His presence like we can that of a friend or family member.

Throughout the book of Psalms, we read the words "God is our refuge" (Psalm 46:1, 91:2). Knowing God is our refuge means God is with us, and we do not need to be afraid. In His presence, we can take comfort. His Word is always reminding us there is safety in His presence.

> The Lord is a strong fortress. The godly run to him and are safe. (Proverbs 18:10 TLB)

There is safety in being known. When we feel known, we feel protected. When our heart embraces the Father's love, we feel known and we feel seen. When we feel seen, we begin to realize what we feel and experience matters. Our lives and pain matter because we matter to God.

When we know our pain matters, we can work through our pain and process it in a way that honors ourselves, God, and the people around us.

How do we process our pain? Our pain may start with someone hurting us or something happening to us. We experience hurt and pain, and we desire for the pain to go away. Yet God invites us in to help us work and process through the pain. He helps us find an answer, accept the pain, and, ultimately, find closure. Remember: As adults, we can experience emotional healing whether someone recognizes our pain or not. Our next course of action will vary depending on circumstances and how God's Word speaks to us about the particular situation we bring to Him. But there is always an invitation from the Father to tend to the broken pieces of our life because He knows us better than anyone else.

Uncomfortable Places

It's important to remember that God is always our safe place, even when life feels like quicksand dragging us deeper under the surface with every step. Remember how, when I felt safe, I started to feel the pain? We're just like a horse that stops running after it feels safe and only then realizes the gash on its leg or the lack of oxygen in its lungs. It might seem that the safe place is responsible for the pain. And there's a part of us that wants to question if God is safe. After all, why would He allow us this pain?

In a moment of questioning, the enemy can come for us and convince us God is the author of sin and its consequences, or God is the author of evil workings.

Our brains try to rationalize the pain. We may try to blame someone or something so the sense of safety can return. If we have an answer, we know the cause and can avoid similar turmoil and/or control the outcome. Without feeling a sense of closure around pain, the wounds stay open for continuous pain to enter, whether invited or not.

Since God's character and nature never change, His Word allows us to close the loop of our pain. Here are a few ways to get started with closing the loop:

1. Pray

James 5:13 encourages us to pray when anyone is suffering: "Is anyone among you suffering? Let him pray." The word *suffering* here can mean enduring hardship, anxiousness, or stress. To pray is to give our feelings to God first, before we go running to someone else. I had to learn the hard way that going to people before God didn't make me feel better. Going to others first only left the wound open, because their words validated what I felt or made me feel shame for what I was experiencing.

For example, when I was dating Bob, my friend Julie told me I was destroying my life and should break up with him. Bob treated me like a contestant on a game show. Would I be the lucky winner for the day or would the other two girls I was competing with take home the prize? I couldn't see the real him because the thought of being alone confirmed the lie that no one wanted me. Julie's words tried to bring comfort to my open wound that couldn't stop bleeding (never-ending loop of pain), but the blood (the pain) kept coming. I didn't want to hear her words because I wasn't ready to face my own feelings.

The piece I was missing was what God said about Bob, my pain, healing, and love. No one was able to take away the pain for me. They were not the ones who created me and know my heart better than me; only God does.

2. Remember

When you pray, ask God to show you the parts of your life that continue to be punctured by the pain we carry. Even though Sarah and I have not talked for many years, the relationship we had affected my life whether she was around or not. Any time Sarah expressed what she did for me when I was young, it was a way to make me do something for her. Her love came with expectations. God had to remind me many times that Sarah's version of love is not His version.

We can remember our pain without the pain forming our identity. David does this beautifully. In Psalm 13:1–2, he says, "How long, O LORD? Will You forget me forever? How long will You hide Your face from me? How long shall I take counsel in my soul, having sorrow in my heart daily? How long will my enemy be exalted over me?" David is honest and specific in his complaints to God. If David, the man after God's own heart, can ask questions, we can too.

3. Have no fear

When God reminds us of the things to pray for, go to His Word to know His character. Knowing His character leads us in the proper direction of healing. Isaiah 41:10 says, "Fear not, for I am with you; be not dismayed, for I am your God. I will strengthen you, yes, I will help you, I will uphold you with My righteous right hand." There is assurance in knowing He is always with us, strengthens us, and upholds us. Coming out of a relationship with Fred, a sociopath, was one of the hardest emotional times in my life. It felt like my entire body was being crushed under the weight of grief. I was grieving who I was, who I turned into, and who I was not. I didn't recognize myself anymore. The end of the relationship compounded years of feeling unworthy. Every day I wrote in my journal, labeling every day "rehab day." I was in rehab with my feelings, walking them out with PJ, my spiritual father (whom I mentioned earlier), and God. I had to not only know God was good but believe He was good to me.

4. Trust

Not only did I have to know God was good and who He was, but I also had to learn I could trust Him with my pain. I had to know He wasn't going to use my pain or my past against me in the future. I wanted to know my pain was taken care of and wouldn't continue to be on trial against who I was becoming as I was healing. I allowed things to happen when dating Ted that I am not proud of. Ted loved to drink. Whenever we went out together, he never knew when to stop, and if I tried to tell him enough was enough, I got the penalty. I was told I was controlling. He convinced me I was in the wrong and he was right, even to the point of him pushing me to get out of his way. Ted was an angry drunk. I questioned if this was something I could trust God with, to not use against me. Then I realized every past moment is taken care of because Jesus went to the cross. When closing the loop of our pain, trusting in God is our safety zone. Trusting in God allows us to open our hands and release what we are white-knuckling over to Him, knowing He will take care of it. Isaiah 26:3–4 is one of my favorite verses, and prompts me to remember I can trust and have peace when I focus on God: "You will keep him in perfect peace, whose mind is stayed on You, because he trusts in You. Trust in the LORD forever, for in YAH, the LORD, is everlasting strength." Remember that to experience the trust and peace God offers, we must keep our minds on Him.

I love knowing there is safety in God's character because He never changes based on how we are on any specific day. He continues to welcome and invite us to sit down at the table He prepares for us with a simple whisper of "Come to me." He hits the key points our hearts need to hear: "Your weaknesses don't make you weak. Where you are weak, I am strong. Even in pain, I am strong in you" (see 2 Corinthians 12:10). Those words continue to remind me of my relationship with God and bring me comfort when I feel weak or not seen. In 2 Corinthians 6:9, Paul tells us that Christians are often "unknown, and yet well known." We may not be known to people, but we are well known by God, the maker of the heavens and the earth. And that should bring us comfort.

My walk to discover safety involved my husband and my spiritual father, PJ. However, you can always find safety in a trusted friend, parent, therapist, or church family to walk with you in the uncomfortable places.

Safe with the Spirit

Experiencing emotional healing comes with understanding. We may hear people say we need to deny our flesh and not sin. While those things are true, there is a slight and subtle change I would like to make. Telling someone to deny their flesh, so the Holy Spirit is more apparent, or not to sin, so they can experience freedom in Christ, tells us to focus on self first, rather than following God first.

Galatians 5:16 says, "So I say, walk by the Spirit, and you will not gratify the desires of the flesh" (NIV). We walk in the Spirit to deny the flesh, not deny the flesh to walk in the Spirit. Our union with God breaks the power of the flesh. We shift our focus from ourselves to God.

We are more able to trust those whom we know love us. A revelation of God's love will make faith naturally abound in us. The degree of love we experience often reveals the depth of faith we will have. God's love is the only love that turns us from our sinful self, because His love is unselfish. All sin is selfish. Therefore, love is the antidote for all sin. His love does what the law could not do. Thank You, Jesus. Partnering with the Holy Spirit will always lead us to life, peace in our soul, and movement toward healing.

God's Word allows us to experience healing, because the selfish part of us is denied when love abounds. There are layers in our healing journey, but those layers will reveal themselves at the depth of love we experience and allow to take over within our hearts. Are we willing to let God's love guide and lead us? Or will we let our selfish desires and struggle for justice and revenge pull us under? Will we accept that we might not find an answer to our why questions because our brains are finite and God is infinite in possibilities?

Before I began to heal, I carried my anger, bitterness, and jealousy as a badge of honor. I often said, "I deserve this much at least" or "They owe me this." Most of the time, I walked around with a self-righteous attitude, as if everyone owed me something for the pain in my life.

After getting married, my husband, Jon, pointed out a behavior I never noticed. Whenever I was in a group of people who disagreed with me or challenged my knowledge or "one-upped" me, I became quiet. My whole body language changed. It was 100-percent visible and noticeable. Jon often said, "Jess, you shut down." I disengaged from the conversation because I thought I was being threatened. I avoided the pain of feeling as though my words didn't matter, which in return made me feel as though I didn't matter and wasn't smart enough. My husband was right. I coped with the insecurity and pain by shutting down. Yet it was an unconscious behavior because my brain signaled a threat.

Using God's lens (His love and Word) to look at our childhood, relationships, or situations doesn't make them smaller, bigger, or insignificant. Viewing them through God's lens allows us to maintain a steadiness in our emotions. Knowing His Word and His love allows us to heal in a way that honors God and honors us (and even the person who may be involved).

———◆◆◆◆◆———

I encourage you to spend some time with the Father as you look through the lens of love. What areas of pain need to be closed and worked on? Do you trust God? When you go to God, do you feel safe with Him? Be honest and accepting of your answer. Remember: This is nothing more than a starting place for understanding why we respond and react the way we do. Answering these questions is not a place where you end. The more I began to understand why I was responding to the situations around me the way I was, with time and as I allowed, God showed me how to change and begin to heal. He showed me how to renew my mind and begin to reframe my stories. Of course, reframing our stories takes our involvement and willingness to go to the hard places. Healing is available to us, but healing is our choice.

Let this be a reminder in the moments when you may feel out of control with your emotions. Many of your responses come through learned behavior that you have to begin to renew to God's truth and what He calls you to do with specific actions.

CHAPTER / TEN

Intentional Healing

I am someone who loves to fix people. Not because I believe they are broken or because I want them as my personal project, but because I know the depth of pain the soul carries when our heart feels tattered and destroyed. Growing up in a trailer with no carpet and using a kerosene heater to stay warm, losing my virginity at the age of twelve, having parents who divorced when I was eighteen, and my dad remarrying gave me a lot of brokenness disguised as confidence and hidden in a fake smile. When I hear people tell victims to simply move on because their past isn't a big deal, my palms want to roll into fists and come to the rescue (of course, in a righteous anger kind of way). In my need to want to fix people, I learned the hard way I am not the Holy Spirit. What my friends, people on social media, and my family feel is real, regardless of whether I think what they feel is logical. All our stories are real to us, but our pain tells the story through a different lens than love does.

Our society way too often approaches trauma like this: Did something bad happen? No worries. God has something better for us anyway. Move on. Is our heart broken? No worries. There are a lot of fish in the sea. Move on. Are we having a bad day? Be positive, think happy thoughts, and everything will go away.

The problem with "moving on" is we can't move through our experiences if we never grieve them. If we never grieve our pain, we stay fractured and broken. The other side to this is completely ignoring what we feel and isolating ourselves, thinking in time everything will go away.

As a society, there isn't much permission to heal completely. Worse, we don't give the Lord permission to show us why we have these feelings in the first place. Moving on only adds one more brick to a foundation that can come crashing down at any second—a lot like the game Jenga.

When a game of Jenga begins, players build a tower of Jenga pieces. To play, players take turns removing pieces from the tower. This leaves the tower with holes, making it less and less stable each time a piece is removed.

The game continues until one piece causes the whole tower to come crashing down.

At birth, we start as a strong tower, feeling invincible. As time goes on, more situations happen and we pile more pieces on top of ourselves as we try to make our way through life—until one day something small sets us off and we lose control completely. Let's gather up all the pieces and begin to look at what made you crash in the first place.

Deliberate Healing

In order to change, we need to know what to change before the Jenga tower of our life crumbles. A few things that get in our way of healing and our relationship with God are our current beliefs about healing and God. Renewing our minds is replacing a lie with the truth. Changing the roots of our thought and redirecting them start with observation. Observation helps us to be intentional with our healing, versus letting time go by and hoping time will heal.

Here are four ways we can begin to be observers of our thoughts:

1. Prayer

Let us pray bold prayers asking the Father to show us areas of our lives we have made an idol, or areas which cause intense emotional responses. He will lead us to the topic, person, or event. Trust Him.

2. Observation

As we pray, we want to begin to observe our thoughts, which is taking them captive. We are holding them without owning them. Imagine sitting in front of a TV screen. You have a remote control in your hand. On the screen, your thoughts are popping up and scanning across the screen. You are the observer with the remote, watching the screen and having full permission to change the station. You have been given the authority through the power of Jesus to cast down every thought to make it obedient to

Christ. Observe the thoughts or stories that do not bring restoration, redemption, or healing. Write them down.

3. Truth

The more we observe, the more patterns we see with our thoughts. These are the moments we get to take God's Word to those thoughts. We may have certain feelings, but what does God's Word say about what we feel? Take the thoughts or stories based on lies and search out the truth to them. What stories in Scripture speak life to the areas feeling dead? Write down the truth.

4. Repetition

Healing from old lies takes time. Uprooting old lies and reaction patterns takes repetition, patience, and grace. We are not practicing positive thinking; we are transforming the lie and pattern at the root. One important step in renewing our mind comes when we can recognize a reaction pattern and bring truth to real-time situations. To keep being persistent, we need to take the truths we know and begin to put them in the places we struggle with those thoughts the most. Maybe on a bathroom mirror? Perhaps on the scale? Would putting them in the car or on the refrigerator be best? We need to see the truth continually.

When we choose to bring a memory to the forefront, we hold a greater ability to renew—to change our minds. When our thoughts are at the forefront, they are pliable. In our fast-paced society and with how busy our minds are, we become like a frustrated person playing Scrabble: staring at a random set of letters, hoping to find a word. The same is true for our thoughts. Sometimes we get busy and don't focus on what we are thinking. Everything we encounter feels frustrating and disorienting. Trying to make sense of what's in front of us causes us to feel emotional overwhelm. Everything we feel, we feel at once, instead of carefully choosing to focus on one feeling. Conscious effort is required to build a word out of a board of random letters. We must choose each piece individually, with intention. May we begin to do the same with our thoughts.

Renewing our minds is not, nor does it feel, easy. As believers, we live in the tension of who we are becoming in Christ and the old unrenewed mind. The tension is a beautiful gift that God has given us: the ability to change our pain, our actions, and our future. Experiencing healing is working through the tension with the Father who has a tender touch to nurture us back to wholeness. When our souls are well, we can be well.

Healing Takes Practice

The worship part of the service had ended. I gathered my things and sat down in the chair next to my husband. The sermon was about to start. I handed Jon his notebook, grabbed my notebook, and made sure we both had a pen. Jon and I both like to journal our thoughts as they come during the sermon. He's a deep thinker and analyzer. I am a deep thinker and feeler. For every page of my notes, Jon may have a few lines in his notebook.

As Jon and I listened to our pastor talk, specific words piqued each of our interests because the topic was one we knew was important. Our pastor was talking about renewing your mind. The words were not new to us, but we heard them differently that day. Reading Scripture is extremely important, but something equally important is what we do with the Scripture we read. The areas of our thought life that are not renewed by God's Word can be conformed to the world (Romans 12:2). To be transformed by the Word of God, we must meditate on His Word.

As I wrote notes and listened to our pastor go deeper on this subject, I looked over at my husband, who was writing more than a few lines. After he finished writing, he tapped my leg and handed over his notebook.

These were the words he wrote:

> I believe we need to practice peace and joy and love and all of these things. To me it's not enough to renew your mind to things. You actually have to practice them too. If God told you that you were going to be a great piano player, it's not something you immediately become good at. If you know we have peace, we could even have every scripture memorized on peace, but if we never practice having peace in our body then our body and mind will be allergic to it as a foreign poison in the body. But, through practice, we cannot just know that we have peace but truly feel it too. Knowledge of the Word is only one aspect. It's the practice that causes the change as well.

He is right.

Over the years, I have witnessed people who can quote Scripture, but then I witness their life and the lack of good fruit. It makes me wonder how much of His Word has penetrated their heart and soul. This way of memorizing and living challenged me to dig deeper into what needs to happen for our soul to change from Scripture, for His Word to truly change our actions, response, and feelings. Here are a few questions to ask yourself:

1. I may know the Scripture, but do I know Him on a personal level? How would I define my relationship with God?

2. Have I put into practice what His Word says? If so, what steps have I taken to continue healing

with the Father? If not, what could I pursue today to put the Word into motion?

3. Am I renewing my mind, or do I want more knowledge? Why is each one of these important?

As we go through this process of renewing and rewiring our minds to believe God's Word for our health and body, we must also begin to put change into practice. Put into practice speaking His Word in your situation and circumstances. God's Word can change our whole physiology.

When we know better, we do better. Are our thoughts producing life or death? Are they leading us to truth or farther from truth? Our soul is the fulcrum—the pivot point. What we pay attention to the most is where our weight will be. Where our focus lies will show us the type of fruit we will yield.

Pursue the Healing

I am the type of girl who, if I have an appointment at 1:00 p.m., tries to cram in everything on my to-do list before I need to leave. I continue to count down the minutes, thinking to myself, *I can get this email taken care of, answer this message, oh and grab something to eat while I watch a little bit of a show on TV with thirty minutes left until my appointment.* I get those things done but find myself in a hurry to get to the appointment, and I feel anxious about being late. Why do I do this to myself? One conclusion is that in the past I saw time as my enemy. I hated running out of time to complete a project. If I did not finish the project, I felt like a failure and should have done more.

Time is a gift, not our enemy. Are we patient with ourselves, and do we express patience in our relationship with God? No one likes to wait around for something to change or for a prayer to be answered. When impatient waiting is involved, time becomes our enemy. We believe we should be farther along in our careers. We believe our bodies should look better by now. Why does this person still rub us the wrong way?

Renewing our minds requires patience and persistence. Shaming ourselves into change will not change us. The time we spend renewing our minds pays off, even when the moments we spend meditating on Scripture don't seem to change anything. Over time we see the change deep in our soul. How do we know if we have changed? Here are some good indicators that God is reshaping our soul to look more like His Son:

1. We have hope.

2. We are quick to find peace in a storm.

3. We live from victory, not as victims.

4. We look for the good in people and not their faults.

5. We are the first to apologize and mean it.

6. We lead with love toward ourselves and others, not with shame.

7. We forgive versus holding grudges.

8. We are quick to wipe off offenses.

9. We are not afraid to give.

10. We laugh more.

We cannot give up the fight. Let us keep the faith (see 2 Timothy 4:7). Change feels hard, but change takes intentional steps every day.

Believing for Healing

I love to read about the woman from Luke 8:43–48 who was bleeding for many years. We witness the intentional pursuit of Jesus despite what the world would have to say about her being in public and bleeding:

> Now a woman, having a flow of blood for twelve years, who had spent all her livelihood on physicians and could not be healed by any, came from behind and touched the border of His garment. And immediately her flow of blood stopped. And Jesus said, "Who touched Me?" When all denied it, Peter and those with him said, "Master, the multitudes throng and press You, and You say, 'Who touched Me?'" But Jesus said, "Somebody touched Me, for I perceived power going out from Me." Now when the woman saw that she was not hidden, she came trembling; and falling down before Him, she declared to Him in the presence of all the people the reason she had touched Him and how she was healed immediately. And He said to her, "Daughter, be of good cheer; your faith has made you well. Go in peace."

Many people have different opinions and perspectives about the encounter between Jesus and this woman. However, there are a few things this passage of Scripture shares that we can apply to our circumstances and situations.

First, a little backstory about the woman: This woman was bleeding for twelve years. In her time, women were considered unclean because of the blood, and thus not allowed to be in public. If she went outside of her home, the woman would have to yell, "Unclean, unclean," so people would move away from her and not touch her. If they touched her, they would be considered unclean as well. So, on top of bleeding for twelve years, she also faced humiliation and a lack of human interaction and touch.

Since our faith comes by hearing the Word of God, this woman had to first hear about Jesus. After she heard about Jesus, she could choose whether to believe that what she heard about Jesus was true or not.

Once she heard the Word, she believed it in her heart and spoke with her mouth: "If only I may touch His clothes, I shall be made well" (Mark 5:28).

Three things happened before she even encountered Jesus:

1. She heard the Word. (She heard about Jesus.)

2. She believed what she heard about Jesus in her heart.

3. She spoke life into what was in her heart. (She used her mouth to confess.)

All kinds of people were touching Jesus as He was walking through the crowd. As the Scripture notes, Peter asks an obvious question: "What do you mean 'Who touched me?' All these people are touching you." As all kinds of people are touching Jesus, we see the bleeding woman meet Jesus with her faith. She encountered Jesus and was made well. (This can also be seen in the book of Acts when people were being laid out on beds hoping to encounter Peter's shadow to be healed.)

Jesus not seeing her with His physical eyes is an example that proves our hard work or striving has nothing to do with our faith in believing. Jesus didn't care about her looks. Jesus didn't care what she did or did not do. Jesus did not care what her past looked like; Jesus cared about the posture and belief in her heart. She had an encounter with Jesus, who is the Word made flesh. She took a risk, crawling on the ground, to touch the hem of His garment. She risked what the world would have done to her (like stone her). The woman believed in her heart what was spoken to her about Jesus. To believe the Word of God for our life is powerful.

The bleeding woman who encountered Jesus that day had spent her money and time on all kinds of doctors, hoping they could make her bleeding go away. Hearing Jesus and encountering His presence are what changed the course of her life, though.

We hear the Word, we believe the Word, and we speak the Word. Now is the time to move in a new direction with our thoughts, speaking those words out loud to ourselves and others, which causes us to walk in a new direction.

Let us be believing believers.

Never Stop Healing

As you believe, mistakes will still happen. Messing up can make us feel like we are derailed from healing, like more should have been done, or we weren't strong enough to handle what came against us. We should not be ashamed of weaknesses, because when we are weak, He can be strong in us. Our life is our witness, and others want to see what truth we stand on. They want to see how we respond and react. The more we are willing to settle into the idea that we don't need to get life perfect, the more freedom we will experience. Perfection is never the goal. Relationship is the goal. Through relationship with God and His Word, we change. This life with Him is beautifully imperfect. Despite the world's desire and pull for perfection, we know perfection doesn't exist deep down.

There is a Jesus people talk about who changes and

transforms. Then there is a Jesus people talk about who doesn't come with the Holy Spirit's power. We could call this the encouragement Jesus, or the "Jesus loves us" message. Although saying Jesus loves us is a sweet reminder and true encouragement, this doesn't always change or penetrate our hearts' deep issues; it is a gospel that doesn't allude to the Holy Spirit's power.

His Word challenges us to get rid of our doubt and unbelief in our dependence on Him. The Bible changes the way the words roll off our tongues against ourselves and our neighbors. The Word of God calls us to higher thinking that leads to a different way of living.

For a long time, I separated the Holy Spirit and me. I observed who He was but not who we were together. All the things I thought disqualified me—things my experiences and the enemy said I should have felt shame for—Jesus covered. He tells us over and over again we were made for good works.

Doing goods works with Him allowed space for the uncomfortable parts of my story and feelings to encounter a Father who said, "There is a different way." In all of our feelings of wanting justice for what happened to us, healing, to feel loved and seen, there is a Father who is calling us up and out by name, saying, "I know you. Come to me. Let me show you the narrow way. I will strengthen you. I will hold you."

The Father's words are kind, never rushing or rude, not condescending, and always understanding. God sent His Son for us to experience not just going to heaven but also abundant life here on earth. Abundant life doesn't mean we won't experience pain or suffering. He left us equipped to handle what comes our way through His Word in this world. We don't have to white-knuckle our way to heaven.

Therefore, faith, time, and patience become our friends and allies. As those who follow Jesus, we continue to stand for the truth, regardless of whether the Word matches what we are experiencing.

We are not going to be perfect, but we can trust in the One who is. His promises of healing and a lifetime of His presence are for you and me. Lean in and listen to the Father saying, "My child, now is the time."

Acknowledgments

I wouldn't be who I am without the transforming power of God, His love, or grace! Thank You, Jesus!

There are many people who helped make this book happen. You read through chapters, gave your opinions, helped me see and paint a clearer picture. You know who you are, and I am forever grateful for your support and love through writing this book.

Thank you to my readers. This book would not be here without your help and answering my questions on social media and through our private conversations in direct messages or email.

Janyre: I am so grateful for your suggestions and edits for this book. This book would not be where it is today without your wisdom and guidance.

Jodi: You have been with me since my first book. Thank you for making my words make sense, and with proper grammar and punctuation in the right spot. The Lord knew I needed someone like you.

The team at Unmutable: You have been wonderful. I am so grateful for all your hard work in making this book come to life. You were a huge part of the process and helped me move through muddy waters when I felt stuck. Thank you!

Jacob: I couldn't ask for a more talented and amazing brother-in-law. Thank you for taking my stick figure sketches and turning it into beautiful artwork.

Alisa: To my writing accountability partner, friend, Mama Keets. Your wisdom, encouragement, and endless Voxers helped this weary soul many times since starting this book. You have been a constant voice of truth reminding me who I am and my call. Thank you!

Stephanie: You know my Jess-isms and still love me. To my very good friend, thank you for listening and always cheering me on. You make me better.

Jon: The celery to my wings you will always be. I couldn't have asked for a kinder, more understanding, and more loving husband. Thank you for always supporting me in all my adventures.

About the Author

Jessica Hottle is a faith-based fitness coach, podcast host, best-selling author, and speaker with a heart for teaching women how to dismantle the lies that keep them from healing and wholeness. She is the author of *Own Your Worth*, *A Worthy Wife*, and *Know Your Worth*, and the host of *What's the Truth?*, a show in which she challenges the way her listeners think so they can change the way they live. Her writing has been featured by *She Works HIS Way*, *Cross Training Couture*, and *Revelation Wellness*. When she isn't writing, speaking, or coaching, you can find Jessica enjoying time with her husband, Jon, being a momma to their three cats, and spending her free time outside (playing golf, hiking, reading, or writing in her journal) whenever she can.

Book Jessica to speak at your event, church gathering, or retreat:

jessicahottle.com/speaking
bookings@jessicahottle.com

Download Your Free Study Guide!

Go deeper with the 10-chapter guide of questions for your healing journey. Great for personal growth, book clubs, and Bible study groups.

JessicaHottle.com/study-guide

Connect with Jessica on social media
Instagram: @jessicahottle
Facebook: jessicahottle22

Other books by Jessica Hottle
Know Your Worth
A Worthy Wife
Own Your Worth